RUBIN

MY LIFE MY ART

AN AUTOBIOGRAPHY
AND SELECTED PAINTINGS
BY
REUVEN RUBIN

WITH AN INTRODUCTION

BY **DR. HAIM GAMZU**

DIRECTOR, TEL AVIV MUSEUM

SABRA BOOKS · FUNK & WAGNALLS · NEW YORK

Page Two
THIS IS THE LAND   1962/64   *oil on canvas* $57\frac{1}{2} \times 38\frac{1}{2}$
collection, Petit Palais, Geneva

Pages Four and Five
RUBIN TODAY IN HIS TEL AVIV STUDIO ON BIALIK STREET
photo Yaacov Agor

Page Eight
SELF-PORTRAIT WITH FLOWER   1921
oil on canvas 38×24
collection of the artist

Designed by Jacob Zim, Tel Aviv
Jacket photograph by Arnold Newman, New York,

SBN 87631–008
Library of Congress Catalog Card Number 74–82694

Contents

To Esther

Introduction

"L'art c'est l'harmonie"
Georges Seurat

Rubin's autobiography takes us through more than seventy years of a life that is multi-colored and exciting. He begins with his Rumanian birthplace in Galati, continues through Falticeni where he spent his youth, Tel Aviv and Caesarea in Israel, where he lives today. In this book, Rubin recounts his background, a home blessed with 13 children, the struggle of parents to feed and clothe them, and his own dream to be an artist. With characteristic directness, Rubin tells of his journeys, his hardships and adventures, his meetings with other artists and interesting people who became his friends and played important roles in his life. Reading these pages, we can almost hear his voice, see his smile, the twinkle in his eye, the expression on his face and the gestures with his hands. These colorful pages form the pageant of a life which reads like a fairy tale.

I have known Rubin for dozens of years. I remember how he looked when I first saw him—his gaunt figure, his curly black hair, and his bony features. His eyes squinted from the glare, and his face was tanned by the sun. Reading Rubin's memoirs makes anyone who knew him then, realize that certain characteristic details were outstanding even in his early childhood: his independence and will-power, his single-mindedness, and his perseverance in striving for a goal which he set for himself—to be an artist and to live in Eretz Israel. These traits paved the way to the crystallization of his individual style in painting, and preserved his originality in a world of various trends and schools of art, which rose and declined in his time.

Rubin did not gain his knowledge in universities, nor did he acquire the techniques of painting and sculpture, woodcarving and etching, tapestries and stage-setting, in the academies of art. Like all talented self-taught artists, he instinctively discovered his own laws of composition, his own color palette, and an original style. In the course of his life, he met many extraordinary people who made their mark in the world of culture, science, theatre, music and literature; never losing an opportunity to learn, he broadened his horizons, absorbed and digested ideas, attitudes and influences. As Maxim Gorky said, "life itself was his university."

Whoever reads Rubin's biography, will find the portrait of an imaginative and energetic man, who never flinches from obstacles, but tries stubbornly to overcome them and succeeds. He has the knack of finding his bearings in all situations, with the ability to get out of difficulties; but no less typical is his restlessness and desire for change, which must be counted among the factors contributing to the constant innovations in his art. These qualities were always balanced by his need for a haven and a love for the land of his people. His productive brush painted its silver-leafed olive woods, the lushness of green orange groves, and the winding trails of Galilee. "I am a Jew and an artist in my own country" writes Rubin, "I feel relaxed and happy there." This feeling is to be found in Rubin's paintings, and distinguishes them from those of most of the Jewish artists who express storms of passion, suffering and torment. He is one of those rare artists who can isolate themselves from daily problems when they stand before their easels with paintbrush in hand, concentrating on their favorite subject. "I paint what I love; my people, my family, my country. To paint is to sing, and every artist must sing his own song," says Rubin, and he has indeed found in the land of Israel the suitable colors to express this love.

Throughout his productive life, Rubin travelled a long road, full of hazard and fateful change, but also rich with wonderful surprise. At the birth of the new State of Israel, the poor Jewish boy, Reuven Zelicovici, was to return to his native Rumania, in the honorable position as the first Minister Pleni-potentiary of Israel. Thus the Government not only recognized the well-known artist, but also the devoted, capable citizen.

His work, rich in imagery, also bears witness to the way the people of Israel has taken root in its soil. His beautiful canvases show ancient olive trees projecting their gnarled branches skyward like priests intoning a blessing. The figures which populate his paintings: rabbis from Jerusalem, sages from Safed, horsemen in the Negev, fishermen on the banks of the Sea of Galilee—all have something magical in their Biblical approach. His hand is sure, his taste is delicate. A hint of poetry mixed with humor tempers the bold and passionate line.

At 76, Rubin is young and full of energy. His eye is sharp, his imagination keen, and he works many hours daily in his studio. Full of confidence in his art and the future of Israel, Rubin pitched his tent in that land, where for over half a century, he continues his emotional dialogue with his work. His life and his work are in complete harmony: that harmony which the painter, Georges Seurat, identified with art.

HAIM GAMZU
Director, Tel Aviv Museum

Biographical Notes

1893   Born in Galatz, Rumania (November 13). At the age of 14, drawings and sketches published in local illustrated magazines and books.

1912   Went to Jerusalem, studied for a year at Bezalel School.

1913/14   Paris; Ecole des Beaux Arts and Académie Collarossi.

1915   Italy; visiting Museums and art treasures.

1916/18   Rumania; doing all kinds of jobs for a living, worked in leather factory.

1919   Studio in Czernowitz; painted war pictures, made sculpture, wrote poetry.

1920   First one-man show at Anderson Gallery, New York, sponsored by Alfred Stieglitz.

1922   Back to Jerusalem; studio in a tent on the sand dunes of Tel Aviv. One-man show, Bucharest, in his "Studio Grivitzi".

1912   Return to Palestine. First artist to hold one-man show in Old Citadel of David, Jerusalem, and Herzlia Gymnasia, Tel Aviv.
Helped create Association of Painters and Sculptors of Palestine, and was its Chairman for 25 years; participated in all their group shows. Published Album of 12 woodcuts, "The Godseekers", made stage designs and costumes for "Jacob's Dream", and "Joske Musikant" (Vilna Troupe).

1924   Exhibition in Bucharest, Caminul Artelor Gallery.

1925   First one-man show in Paris, Bernheim Gallery. (Catalogue text by Edmond Fleg).

1926   Annual exhibition of Artists Organization, Jerusalem. Painting, "My Family" receives Lord Plumer Prize, presented to Tel Aviv Museum.

1927   One-man show in Tel Aviv. (Catalogue text by Chaim Nachman Bialik).

1928   Exhibition in Paris, Druet Gallery. Painting, "Village of Sumeil", purchased by French Government.
Exhibition in Tel Aviv
Exhibition in New York, New Gallery. Acquisitions by Brooklyn Museum, Newark Museum. (Catalogue text by George S. Hellman).

1930   Married Esther Davis of New York.
First one-man show in London, Arthur Tooth Gallery. Acquisitions by Manchester Museum, Ben Ury Society.

1930/31   Exhibition in New York, Montross Gallery.
Exhibition in Jerusalem. French Consulate.
Stage decor for Habima and Ohel Theatres.

1932   Opening of Tel Aviv Museum with one-man Rubin Exhibition.

1936/37   One-man show in Jerusalem, Bezalel Museum.
Exhibition in Jerusalem, Steimatzky Gallery.
Exhibition in Tel Aviv, Bach Gallery.

1940/45   Exhibition in New York, (1940), Milch Gallery.
Acquisition, "Flute Player", Museum of Modern Art, N.Y.
Exhibition in Los Angeles, (1941) Hatfield Galleries.
Acquisition, Los Angeles County Museum.
Exhibition in San Francisco, (1941) Gumps Gallery.
Exhibition in New York, (1942) Bignou Gallery.

Exhibition in Los Angeles, (1944) Hatfield Galleries.
Acquisition, Santa Barbara Museum.
Exhibition in New York, (1945) Lilienfeld Gallery.
Tour Exhibition of 30 paintings (1944–46)
  Oklahoma Art Center, Okla.; Witte Museum, Texas; Philbrook Museum, Tulsa, Okla.; Wichita Art Museum, Kan.
  First Purchase Prize by San Antonio Museum, "Jerusalem".
Awarded Degree of Doctor Honoris Causa, Jewish Institute of Religion, N.Y.

1942   Exhibition in New York, Museum of Modern Art, "Portraits of the Twentieth Century".

1945   Birth of son David, in New York.

1947   Exhibition in Tel Aviv Museum.

1948   Stage designs and costumes for "Hershele Ostropoler" (Ohel). "Day and Night", "Noah" (Habima).
Appointed Minister Plenipotentiary to Rumania by the new Israel Government; returned to Israel in 1950.

1948/1950/1952   Exhibited at Venice Biennale.

1952   Birth of daughter Ariella, in New York.

1952/54   One-man show in New York, (1953) Grace Borgenicht Gallery. Los Angeles, (1954) Hatfield Galleries. Charlotte, N.C., (1954) Mint Museum; Nashville, Tenn. (1954) Museum of Nashville.
Participated in group show "Seven Israel Artists", Metropolitan Museum of Art, N.Y. Institute of Contemporary Art, Boston.

1960   Participated in group show, Paris, Musée National D'Art Moderne. Museum Acquisitions: "Goldfish Vendor", and "Les Grenades".

1961   Album, 12 Lithographs, "Visages d'Israel" published by Jacomet, Paris. (Text by Florent Fels and Dr. Haim Gamzu).

1955   Retrospective Exhibition in Tel Aviv Museum (Catalogue text by Dr. Eugene Kolb, Director).

1957   One-man show in London, Ohana Gallery (Catalogue text by Eric Newton).

1958   Participated in group show, London, Arts Council of Britain.

1962   Retrospective Exhibition, New York, Wildenstein Gallery. Retrospective Exhibition, Los Angeles, Hatfield Galleries. Retrospective Exhibition, Tucson, Ariz., Rosequist Gallery.

1964   Prize of the City of Tel Aviv for life's artistic achievement.

1966   Commission for painting in Knesset, Parliament in Jerusalem, for room of the Cabinet, "Glory to Galilee".
Retrospective Exhibition — 50 Years of Painting — Israel Museum, Jerusalem and Tel Aviv Museum. (Catalogue text by Dr. Haim Gamzu, Director).
First one-man show, Geneva, Galerie Motte.

1967   First one-man show, Palm Beach, Norton Gallery of Art. Acquisition of "Musical Interlude in Caesarea" by Museum.

Rubin in Jerusalem 1912

Rubin in Bucharest, 1917

Rubin Painting, 1934. Musicians of Safed, Collection, Beth Shalom, Jerusalem

Rubin and wife Esther, 1951. Photo: Anna Riwkin-Brick

Rubin painting his son David in Tel Aviv studio, 1951

Rubin family, 1963, in Tel Aviv studio. Photo: Erde

Childhood and School Days

The main street of the Jewish quarter in the city of Galatz, on the Danube, was called simply "the Jewish street," and it was on that street that I was born in 1893. It was really nothing but a passway, narrow, without sidewalks or pavements, and faintly lighted by two or three gas lamps. In the summer the dust collected in heaps and in the winter the street became a river of water and mud. We lived in a housing compound in an empty lot called a *maidan*, which was surrounded by about a dozen small synagogues. There were synagogues in front of our house, to its right, and to its left, and at the back there was an opening onto the *maidan* where all the garbage of the neighborhood was thrown.

We were a large family. My mother was never quite sure of the number of children, but she used to say that there were thirteen or fourteen. I was the eighth or ninth, and four or five were born after me. Of us all, only two are living today. Our house consisted of a few small rooms with earthen floors where we slept two or three in a bed, which consisted of two planks of wood, occasionally covered with a mattress.

The house was always full of people. My father also came from a family of thirteen, and it was seldom that there were not uncles and aunts or cousins staying with us, while neighbors were constantly dropping in. I can recall it being said that "where there are so many, another two or three make no difference."

To me, my father was the most interesting person in the whole world and I looked at him with awe. In our little beehive of activity he went around calmly, never excited, always humming a Hassidic tune in his rich, full voice. He was a tall, heavy-looking, handsome man, with blue eyes and blond hair. How did he manage to make a living? How was he able to fill the many mouths with bread? He never had a steady job but was always busy giving advice to the people who came to him as to a wise rabbi and, in fact, they called him "Reb Joel." His full name was Joel Zelicovici.

He took care of the little synagogue next door to us, acting as *hazan* (cantor), *shamas* (beadle), and general factotum. What with taking care of the synagogue and giving advice, nobody knew how he found the time to make any money. His friends used to say that he had an excellent head on his shoulders, and if only he would take a real job or go into business, he would make a lot of money. But my father used to reply that he did not want to be a slave to money: "I manage somehow. God loves me and sends me what I need. You don't see my children going naked or without food."

What he truly looked forward to were the Jewish holidays, Friday evening, and the Sabbath, when he could let his voice rise in prayer and sing with all his heart. People used to stand by the windows of the

SELF-PORTRAIT 1920 *bronze*
collection, Mr. and Mrs. Bernard Weinberg, Paris
photo by Zafrir

synagogue to listen to him, so beautiful and full of feeling was his voice.

My mother was a little woman, the daughter of a rabbi. She was married at the age of fifteen to this man whom she had never seen before. She told me what a great moment it was when at the wedding ceremony she saw for the first time the fair, fine-looking young man who had been chosen as her husband. She had been afraid she would be bound to a cripple or a blind man. She had a sunny, happy personality with a fine sense of humor and was always willing to be of help to anybody. Everyone called her "Aunt Feige" (Fanny).

My mother introduced into the house a younger sister, Etta, to help with the many chores. Etta was fair and slender, and with her two long braids she looked like a young peasant girl. It was she who brought me up. Soon after I was born, she laid her hand on my head and said, "Nobody is going to touch my little Rivile except me." I continue to bless her memory for all the love and devotion she gave me, because I was a small, puny infant who needed a lot of attention.

My first memory, when I was no more than two years old, had to do with the impact of color. I was awakened in the middle of the night by the sound of an explosion and screams. My mother carried me out in a blanket to the wooden balcony in front of our house, and I saw an enormous fire with smoke rising into the sky. A nearby alcohol factory was burning, and bottles and barrels were exploding, throwing our poor community into a panic as they thought the end of the world had come. But I started to jump up and down and to clap my hands at the wonderful, colorful sight. Everyone looked with wonder at the child so gleefully enjoying the huge fire.

It was the custom for the children of the Jewish quarter to go to *heder* (religious school) at the age of three. There the child learned to read the Bible, the prayers, and the commentaries, and if he had a good capacity to learn, the world was open to him. He could become a *hazan* (cantor), a teacher, even a rabbi. What more can a Jewish child aspire to? So, at the age of three I was sent off to *heder*, to Rebbe Moishele. Small as I was, I went unaccompanied. I was just told to go "around the corner, down to the left, the fourth house, and there you'll find Rebbe Moishele. Sit down and listen quietly and come home in the afternoon."

Some food was packed in a little napkin: a piece of bread, an apple, a green onion, a hard-boiled egg and a few olives. I can still see myself with my little bundle in hand, dressed in a suit belonging to one of my older brothers, walking along slowly.

It's interesting to walk along a road all by yourself when you're only three. There is always something to catch the eye, a little stick to take in your hand, a piece of paper with printing on it, a broken piece of blue glass, a few little stones. After a hundred steps my pockets are bulging. Maybe I should eat something? I sit down at a corner near a bakery, where a donkey stands with two paniers full of bread. He must find the smell of my onion appetizing, for he comes over and gobbles up my lunch. But

I only smile at the donkey and go off to the *heder* without my bundle.

I find the *heder* and enter a room which contains about twenty to thirty children and a little man with a big beard and a high voice, who keeps running about while his wife tries to tidy up the place. Then from time to time the rabbi calls the children to him as he sits in a corner, and together they chant certain lessons. Nobody takes any notice of me and nobody asks me what I am doing there. I find a piece of brick covered with plaster. I look at the rabbi with his glasses on top of his nose and I take the piece of broken glass from my pocket and scratch a profile into the white plaster. Astonishing! The plaster is white and yet when you scratch it you get a red line!

The rabbi's wife tells me it is time to go, and slowly I wend my way home. My family ask me what I have been doing all day but I am too tired to answer. Then, when I am picked up to be taken to bed, all my treasures fall out of my pockets. Someone picks up the brick with my drawing on it. "Look, it is Rebbe Moishele!" I had actually drawn a likeness that could be recognized. My first day at *heder*, my first drawing, and my first artistic success!

After that I enjoyed going to *heder*, chanting and intoning the texts with the other boys, learning first the alphabet and then to read, and listening to the stories of the Bible. But especially did I revel in the discovery that one could draw with charcoal: the joy of tracing black lines on white. How happy I was when I could find a wall to cover with my scribblings.

I never lacked subjects. In the summer there was the shoemaker sitting cobbling in the street, the water-carrier with his two pails; in the spring there was the *matza* being baked and then carried around in high tiers; *Shavuot*, when the dusty acacia trees near the synagogue were covered with clusters of yellow flowers; *Succoth*, and the building of the outdoor tabernacles with their greenery and hanging fruit. There was always something for my eyes to observe and my hands to draw. The Jewish quarter was full of life and movement. It was rich in all that money cannot buy.

For a while I was the youngest in the family and the tiny plaything of all the others. What I thoroughly enjoyed were the Jewish holidays, when my father discarded his old, torn clothes and dressed himself in his Sabbath robes. It seemed to me that he had become a prince, especially when he took me on his knee and sang the Hassidic melodies and prayers. It was only much later, in 1921, when I went to New York to hold an exhibition there and heard Chaliapin in "Boris Godunov," that I realized how wonderful my father's voice was. Chaliapin's voice recalled that of my father.

I loved the High Holy Days, with the ritual, the elegant clothes, the pomp—if one can apply such a word to what was, after all, only grand in comparison with our drab, everyday life. But I also loved the street gangs, the fights, the excitement, the rivalry. It was in the Jewish street that the gangsters met every Saturday afternoon.

The members of the different gangs, formed according to nationality, appeared in their Sunday best, perfumed and neat, with their hair plastered down, and tried to flirt with the Jewish girls. There was Yanosh, six-feet-eight, a giant of a man with a red mustache and a bald head, although he was only twenty-five. He was the terror of the whole street, and the only person he showed any respect for was my mother. He even allowed her to scold him and to give him advice, and he in turn would bring her presents of fruit and chocolate, probably stolen.

Then there was Ghitza Cretzu (the curly-haired), a good-looking man with a beautiful smile and a little black mustache. The police were aware that he was a deserter from the army, but they were too afraid of his gang to arrest him. There was roly-poly Niko Dop (the cork), a thief rather than a gangster, whose quick and violent temper made us all afraid of him. Tanasaki, head of the Greek gang, was known for always carrying two "flick-knives" in his pockets.

These gangs were always at war with one another, either over the girls or over stolen property, and the Jewish street was usually the scene of their fights. The proceedings began with a parade of the gangsters and their girl friends. In the evening they would visit the wine shops and public houses in the vicinity and then around midnight the fights would start. People ran to their homes and bolted the doors. Shots and shouts and screams could be heard, but nobody ventured out. The next morning, wounded and even some dead would be found in the street, but the police could never learn from anybody why or how the fights occurred or who was involved.

The gangsters liked to write letters to their girl friends and this is where I came in. I was the only one of my family who had sufficient schooling to write Rumanian correctly, and time and again a gangster would call on Rivile to write a love letter. When I decorated the page with a drawing of a little bird or a flower, I was paid extra. It was amazing how these gangsters appreciated a clean page of writing with a decoration on it. It seemed to have some symbolic significance for them.

I was six years old when I began to ask my parents to send me to school, but they were too ignorant to know how to set about enrolling me. So, small as I was, I went on my own to the primary school in the neighborhood, on which was written, School No. 1. Timidly I made my way into the office and explained to the official that I wanted to go to school. He treated me kindly, being sorry for the little boy who was so anxious to learn. He asked me my name and date of birth and told me to bring him my birth certificate.

I did not quite understand what he meant, but I asked my parents to tell me the date of my birth. It took them about an hour to work out the year, but they could not recall the exact date. They only remembered that at the time, it had been cold and rainy, and so they decided it must have been in November. Then my Aunt Etta pointed out that "13" was a lucky number and thus the date of my birth was established as November 13. I passed on this information to the school official and he accepted me as a pupil. That is how my school life commenced.

Nobody at home was interested in what I was learning or with whom. What was insisted upon was that I continue my Hebrew studies, so every Friday afternoon and Sunday morning I had lessons with a rabbi who came to the synagogue. I never returned to the *heder* and Rebbe Moishele.

At school I soon became known as the boy who could draw and do attractive lettering, and I can still remember how proud I was when I was asked to write announcements of special events for the class. My brother Baruch, who was a year older than I, decided that he too wanted to go to school and it was through him that I met a boy who was actually able to read the newspaper. This boy sent some of my drawings to a children's newspaper, which published a number of them and, what is more, actually paid for them.

Drawing lessons, of course, were beyond consideration. I never even saw a colored reproduction till I was ten years old. Then an older friend of my brothers brought a catalogue from the Louvre to show us. What a sensation to see a painting reproduced in color! My ambition was awakened. But how could I manage to obtain colors to paint with? In our house filled with children, relatives and neighbors wandering in and out, and with endless discussions about family matters, who had the interest to talk to a small boy about his craving to paint?

It is true that I was only a child, but yet I had a constant heartache because of the indifference with which my drawings and sketches were treated. My poor mother, always busy with her cooking and baking and her striving to stretch out our scanty means, could see no sense at all in my drawings, and whenever she found a piece of paper with a sketch on it, she would use it to wrap up a slice of cheese or a slab of butter or to cover a pot of milk. I still remember how bitterly I used to cry when I found one of my drawings with a ring of fat or blotches of milk on it. Nobody understood the reason for my tears. After all, what is a piece of used paper? And I, poor mite, could not explain what had upset me.

Then a boy at school told me that his older sister was taking painting lessons. He was very proud that she was learning to paint flowers on velvet. I was thrilled and asked him to take me to watch how she did it. He stole two little tubes of oil paint from her—yellow and blue—and promised to give them to me if I would paint a picture for him. How I enjoyed handling those tubes of color, squeezing them in my fingers and seeing the paint run out! I remember that I painted him a picture of a lighthouse by the sea, although I had never actually seen one. But I had the blue paint for the sea and I knew that a lighthouse sent out yellow rays. The half-used tubes of paint I kept in my treasure box till they dried up.

I remember my childhood years as being overshadowed by the worry of how to keep warm in winter and where to find a decent shirt to wear. The primary school of three grades was not far from our house, so that even if it rained or snowed I could still run back without getting

Overleaf: FIRST SEDER IN JERUSALEM 1950 *oil on canvas* 50½ × 64 collection of the artist

too wet and cold. But the fourth grade was in another school, about two miles away, on the other side of the city. And if my clothes became soaked, there was always the problem of finding something to change into. My father tried hard to feed and dress his brood, but it seemed as if the tremendous number of his dependents overwhelmed him, and he did not have the ability or the energy to find a job which would give him a sufficient income.

Although only a little boy, I was conscious of his worries and doubts and longed to be able to help him. I was his favorite child and he would often take me by the hand and caress me. When I looked up at this tall, handsome man with his broad forehead and shiny eyes, I used to feel as if an angel had touched me and taken away all my childish fears. I think he felt the warmth of my attachment, and sometimes, instead of telling me stories, he would speak of his troubles and difficulties. This seemed to ease his mind, although I hardly understood what he meant.

The great holiday in our house was Passover, when spring came with its clear sky and air and the snow and rain disappeared. Then our shabby home was cleaned and whitewashed and my mother and sisters put down fresh loam on the floors. How beautiful the house seemed to me then, with its white walls, which I often covered with my drawings only to get a thrashing later for defacing them. Before Passover my father always managed to bring home a long length of cloth given to him by friends who worked in a factory. I call it cloth because we had suits made from it, but actually it was the cheapest and shoddiest of materials. I hated the very feel of the stuff and always protested at having to wear a suit made from it, but my brothers laughed at me for being so "particular." My father would call in a neighbor, Mr. Bukanetz, a little fellow with a big paunch, to make the suits. It was said that he was really a receiver of stolen goods, but he was willing to undertake any activity, even tailoring. He did not bother with taking measurements but just went off with the material and returned with the number of suits ordered. Naturally they did not fit any of us, but we had to wear them anyway, in case we should bring discredit to our father's house by letting the town know that he was too poor to buy suits for us. Passover was also the time when the family got new shoes. My feet seemed to grow more quickly than anyone else's, and it seemed as if every few months my shoes became too small and my big toe pushed itself out. I still remember how, before going off to school, I would put blacking on my big toe to make it appear part of the torn shoe.

In the winter of 1903, when I was in the fourth grade, I read in a newspaper that the great Yiddish writer Sholom Aleichem was in Galatz to lecture and give readings from his works. I had heard people discussing his stories and had heard some of them read aloud. I decided I would go to the lecture hall, but as I could not afford a ticket I had to wait outside. When Sholom Aleichem left the hall, I went up and spoke to him. He seemed very amused when I told him that I was in the fourth grade and had organized a reading club, and as we boys had no money to come and hear him would he perhaps come to our school and read to us?

Looking back, I cannot understand where I got the courage to approach such a famous writer. But at the time it came naturally to me. Sholom Aleichem, like the fine man he was, took my request seriously and promised to come on a certain afternoon to the address I gave him. With feverish anxiety I made arrangements for the great day and persuaded the boys to each bring a candle, as it already was dark at five o'clock. On the appointed afternoon, Sholom Aleichem arrived as promised and sat with us boys for an hour in our cold classroom, reading to us "The Penknife," a story for children, by the light of the candles.

It was when I was about ten years of age that I began to long for holiday time. School ended in June and then I was free to roam about the streets and collect colorful stones and pieces of material. I did not care for the noisy games of the other youngsters and spent most of my time alone. I felt happy running barefoot through the dust, entranced by the appearance of the people and animals in the streets and by the shapes of the trees.

I was always making sketches. It became known that there was a boy in the Jewish street with a gift for drawing and making decorations. After I had designed a front cover for the reader's desk in my father's synagogue, embodying a menorah (eight-pronged candlestick), lions and foliage such as I had seen in old books, the men in the other synagogues approached my father to ask that I decorate their synagogues too. How proud I was to do such work, never thinking for an instant of asking for any reward.

At *Shavuot* (Pentecost—festival of the first fruits), it was I who was asked to arrange the decorations, with flowers and branches of trees. But never shall I forget how on one *Shavuot* I came into the synagogue carrying my greenery and had just started to hang the leafy branches when, what did I see?—Mordechai, the beadle, hanging from a candelabra! It was my first contact with death. Trembling, I ran home and told my family that Reb Mordechai was hanging from a candelabra with his tongue protruding, and when I touched him, he swung to and fro. It was never discovered why the old man had hanged himself just before the beautiful holiday of *Shavuot*, but some people said that it was because his wife had left him. After that experience, I could never again bear to decorate a synagogue.

The great joy of the summer holidays was that we could spend so much time in the open air. There was a long, wooden balcony around the house where all the brothers slept on the hot, stuffy nights. What a wonderful time we boys had, throwing pillows at one another, laughing and talking. One summer morning a friend of one of my brothers came to tell me that I should come to school quickly as I had won a prize. Half asleep, I ran with him to school, and there at the entrance was a big notice stating that Reuven Zelicovici had been awarded the first prize for achievement and that the ceremony, with a crowning, was to take place in the big hall of the public school later in July. All the family were very impressed, but my thoughts were occupied with what I would wear, as I had no suitable clothes and was ashamed to appear in my usual rags. My older sister said that she had an old white dress from which she could make me a sailor suit. I did not want to be dressed as a sailor, nor did the suit fit me. I was so upset that I was afraid to see myself in the mirror. But my pleadings were of no avail, and I was forced to wear it.

When the great day arrived, my family accompanied me to school and we were all surprised to find it quiet, with nobody about. Then, on a window, I found an announcement which explained that the celebration had been postponed for a month as the great Dr. Theodor Herzl had died that very day!

When the day for the crowning ceremony at last came around, I had no more heart for it and no pleasure in the praise and presents. The family took me to a photographer so that I could be photographed wearing my crown. I refused to stand still and had literally to be held in place. When the daguerreotype was shown me I did not recognize myself and burst out laughing. It very soon got lost and was not seen again. This portrait of me was the first photograph ever taken in my family. The walls of our house were bare—no pictures, no photographs. I remember that when my grandfather first saw a photograph which my brother sent us from America, he could not understand what it was but kept turning it around, saying, "I can't read something like this."

After I had completed the four grades of primary school, none of the family thought that there was anything more for me to learn. But I was filled with a burning desire for knowledge. Some of my friends had entered the Jewish Community High School, but the fees were too high for my father. I wept every day, saying that I must continue school, that I must learn and develop my mind, while my whole family joined together in thinking that I was not normal and that further education was quite unnecessary.

One day, one of my cousins from another city came to visit us on his way to study law in Bucharest. He told me that since I had finished primary school with a first prize, I was entitled to a government scholarship even if I were a Jew, and that I should be admitted to the Government High School free. I was very excited and immediately applied to the Ministry of Education in Bucharest. The application was returned with the information that it had to be signed by three Rumanian citizens who could testify to the moral and social standing of my parents.

Now I was faced with the problem of finding the three Rumanian citizens, because, as always, I had to do everything myself. First I thought of the postman. He was a Rumanian citizen; he duly signed. Next was the street cleaner, who was likewise a Rumanian citizen. He could not write so he affixed his thumb mark on the application.

Now for the third witness. I knew that near our street there lived a Rumanian citizen in a big house, and I was told that I should go to see

ENCOUNTER 1919 *oil on canvas* 27½ × 37½ collection, Mr. and Mrs. A. Polany, Tel Aviv

him and beg him to sign the document. I gathered my courage and went to his house. I rang the bell. When the door was opened, a big dog ran out and bit me. I fell down bleeding, but kept my application high in the air so that it would not get dirty. The man of the house, hearing the commotion, came to the door. He was very kind to me and had my foot bandaged.

He was amazed to learn of the reason for my visit and the rest of the household started to laugh at the shabby little Jewish boy who had dared to come to a strange house with such a request. Nobody even said that they were sorry about my being bitten by the dog. Eventually, however, the man did sign the document. So home I came, my foot bandaged, but my application duly signed by three Rumanian citizens.

After some weeks a telegram arrived from the Ministry of Education in Bucharest. It advised me that my application was approved and that I should present myself without delay at the Vasili Alexandri Lyceum, as the school term had already started.

Having found out where the school was located I went there, asked for the first form, entered the classroom and seated myself on a bench. The class consisted of Rumanian Gentile boys only. Jews did not customarily go to such schools and the boys, brought up in a tradition of anti-Semitism, did not want to sit near me. They started to push and pummel me and at last I found a seat up against the wall.

There was no day on which I did not shed tears. But I did not stay away from school, even though nobody took any notice of me. The teacher did not call me to the blackboard or question me, and my name was not included in the roll call.

One day a problem in mathematics came up and the teacher asked if anyone could solve it. I raised my hand and was at last called to the blackboard. I gave the correct answer and the teacher seemed to recognize my presence for the first time. When he asked me how I had come to be in the class, it came out that I was not even registered for that particular form. I was told to find out where I really belonged. Then I learned that I had been registered for another class, and since I had not answered to my name in the roll call for over a month, my name had been removed altogether. I burst into tears, and the school secretary, feeling sorry for me, told me that I would be registered again in the proper class. But I must go and introduce myself to the teacher and, moreover, I must get a school uniform.

Again I went home weeping. How could my father possibly afford to have a school uniform made for me? Again my sister came to my rescue. She had an old black dress from which she could make the uniform. How successful the suit was can be judged by the laughter that greeted my appearance in class. Probably I did look rather ridiculous, but I did not allow the derision and contempt of my classmates to keep me away from school. And after some time, both the teachers and the students admitted that I was a good pupil, and my drawings brought me a certain degree of attention. At the end of the year I received a gold medal from the Ministry of Education.

During this first year at the lyceum I came into closer contact with nature. One of the boys, the son of a rich man, became quite friendly with me and invited me to spend a weekend at his parents' country home. A Jewish boy asked to spend the weekend in the home of wealthy Rumanians? This was an unheard-of event, and my family and the Jewish street as a whole could not get over it. When at length my friend arrived in a carriage driven by a uniformed coachman, the whole street was agog. Such a carriage and pair of horses had never before been seen in the Jewish street!

The country house was about two hours' ride from the city and on arrival I was warmly greeted by my friend's parents; they were glad to see him accompanied by a schoolmate, for he was an only son, their other child being a daughter. My stay in that house was like a dream. The trees, the green lawn, the flowers, the various farm animals—a new world which I never knew existed was opened to me. I spent two days there and came home convinced that, after all, paradise does exist on earth.

I spent only two years at the Vasili Alexandri Lyceum. Being the only Jewish boy among a class of forty Rumanians, I felt like an outcast all the time. Though I do not recall ever having been physically molested or beaten, I felt out of place and awkward, a stranger among these youngsters who were at home and at ease in a way I could not be. They always tried to make me ashamed of being Jewish, throwing insults in my face and not allowing me to take part in their games. I did not find any more sympathy on the part of the teachers. Some of them were outspoken anti-Semites who, when they mentioned Jews, invariably denigrated them.

By nature I was very sensitive to injustice or insult and maybe I had an overdeveloped feeling of pride, with the result that my two years at the lyceum were years of torment and mental suffering. A couple of the boys were a little less unfriendly than the others. But on the whole, I passed the formative years of eleven to thirteen in an atmosphere of disdain and disparagement, which undoubtedly left a permanent mark on me.

There was one teacher especially, the geography teacher, whose spiteful remarks I cannot forget to this day. Although it was generally admitted that I drew better than anyone else in the class, this teacher always dismissed my aptitude as being of no importance. One day he asked the boys to come to the blackboard to draw a particular map, and he had to include me too. For some reason I felt an impulse to defy him, and when he told me to depict Europe, I produced my colored chalks and drew a magnificent complex world map, with blue lines for the rivers and seas, brown for mountains, and green for the plains. The other boys were delighted, but the teacher was boiling with annoyance.

Suddenly he asked me, "And where is the North Pole?" Perhaps I

MEAL OF THE POOR   1920   *oil on canvas*   36 × 29   collection, Mrs. T. Amir, Tel Aviv

did not hear the question correctly, for instead of the North Pole I drew the Arctic Circle. "But Palestine, you know where that is?" he asked.

I took the question at its face value and drew that part of Asia which contains Palestine. This drew roars of laughter from the class, and only then did I realize that the teacher had asked the question in a spirit of mockery. With tears in my eyes I threw the chalks on the teacher's table and ran back to my desk. He was outraged by my behavior and I was at once called to the secretary's office for an explanation. I do not know where I got the courage, but I would not accept the teacher's accusations and instead launched into a loud peroration about my people and Palestine.

The teacher's purpose of calling me to the secretary's office as a punishment did not have that effect at all. After my outburst I was simply sent back to the classroom and told not to be "cheeky," and that was all. I felt as if I had gained a great victory.

Although this was only a small incident, it was an important event in my young life. Firstly, it made a decided impression on the class, which found an echo throughout the school, and the satisfaction I got from speaking my mind and not taking insults quietly had a bracing effect on my whole character.

It was not long before I realized that this little incident had become known in the upper grades, mainly among the few Jewish boys who had been admitted to the lyceum because of high scholastic attainments or rich connections. One day during recess, as I was standing about watching the other boys playing, a student in the eighth form, of about seventeen, with a sensitive, thin face, came over to me and asked if I was the boy who had defied the geography teacher. He said that he was also a Jew, that he was finishing high school that year and was going to go to a university to study medicine. He gave me his address and asked me to come to his house the following Sunday afternoon.

I felt very pleased at having become so well-known in a school of more than 800 pupils. I had always dreamt of becoming known, but only through my drawings. However, it seemed that artistic fame did not come easily; my outspoken comments in a moment of daring had done more to bring attention to me than any drawings I could have done.

I eagerly awaited Sunday and felt very proud at having a friend of nearly eighteen. The young man, whose family name was Schechter, was the son of a Talmudic scholar living in a modest little house. I met his mother and a younger sister of about thirteen. This girl was the first of the opposite sex to attract me: I found her beautiful, and dressed with exquisite taste. I could not help thinking that she had dressed herself with particular care in order to impress me.

Also present were a number of youths, including some boys from our school. Schechter explained that they comprised an organization of Jewish schoolboys, all of whom were proud of being Jews, and that their aim was to develop a feeling of human dignity and self-respect among their own people. They were not Zionists but merely a group of young people with eager minds who wanted to break through the restricted, mentally narrow atmosphere of Jewish ghetto life.

I was introduced as a sort of celebrity and they all congratulated me on the stand I had taken in challenging the anti-Semitic geography teacher. I felt very proud and happy. As a reward for my "courage," Schechter announced that I had been unanimously accepted as a member of the group, in spite of the fact that I was not yet thirteen, the lowest age for acceptance. To become a full member I would have to prepare a speech, to be delivered within the next three months, to demonstrate my intellectual capacities. The subject chosen was, "My Ideals in Life." In the meantime, I could attend the weekly Sunday meetings, but the matter would have to be kept secret because the school authorities would consider the organization subversive, and, if found out, we would be expelled.

My school life continued to be miserable, and although I excelled at drawing, the drawing teacher never gave me good marks but always criticized my "unorthodox" way of doing things. I wanted to leave the lyceum at the end of the first year, but the Jewish high school would not admit me without payment, and my family could not afford the fees. Not only did I have to contend with the dislike of the boys and staff, but I did not have the money to buy even the necessary school books. I used to make my own exercise books out of grocery wrapping paper, in which I would write the teachers' questions and the boys' replies, and for which I invented a sort of hieroglyphics. Somehow I always seemed to know the lessons, but it was certainly a very exhausting way of learning. The only happy day of my week was Sunday, when I met with the "group" and received some encouragement from these friendly comrades.

Then, quite unexpectedly, at the close of my second year at the lyceum I was called for an interview by the heads of the Jewish high school, who had heard about me. They informed me that, as an exception, I would be accepted as a non-paying pupil. Now life began to be brighter; I was no longer weighed down by anti-Semitic attacks. I got on well with the other students and it was here that I met a boy who became a great friend, Ludwig Feldmann. The son of a well-known doctor who was the head of the Jewish community, he was a quiet, dreamy boy, and a very gifted violinist. It was through him that I first heard the names of Beethoven, Brahms and Mozart and began to develop a taste for music.

I spent many evenings in the cultivated, intellectual Feldmann household, where I met people and heard conversation very different from that of our poverty-stricken ghetto street. For the first time I entered a proper bathroom with hot and cold water running from a faucet. Many a Sunday morning did I find my friend lounging in a bathrobe and bedroom slippers—things I did not know existed. I used to go for long walks with him while he talked about music and musicians, opening my mind to this new world.

In later life I had occasion to hear his beautiful playing from time to time, and when I visited Bucharest after World War I, I found him studying with the noted Georges Enescu. Now, as I write these lines, I hear that Feldmann is considered to be one of Rumania's outstanding composers, after having been concertmaster of the Bucharest Symphony for many years.

These meetings in my early youth with boys like Schechter and Feldmann encouraged me to think for myself and gave me the spiritual strength to develop and broaden my horizons. Life at home continued to be narrow, poor and hard, and I had arrived at an age when I felt I should earn a little money of my own so that at least I could buy myself a pair of shoes or the materials I needed for drawing and school. I still remember with gratitude my mathematics teacher, who used to recommend me as a coach for children who were backward in this subject. Through him I was able to earn some much-needed money.

After finishing four grades of high school, I felt I must leave and get a regular job. It was difficult to find somebody who would hire a boy not yet fifteen, but it so happened that the father of a friend of mine had a big wine shop and he engaged me to help in the office. It was not very long before I took over the running of the whole office and earned higher wages. At the same time, I went on studying with the help of books borrowed from my friends still at school, and in this way I was able to go through the fifth and sixth grades.

But, physically and mentally this life was too fatiguing for a growing boy, and the job in the wineshop was no outlet for my intellectual energy. However, this energy eventually found release in my contributing to a magazine which our group produced, for I was beginning to be interested in literature and poetry. I can still recall how on cold winter nights I used to read late by candlelight, devouring one book after another. But somehow or other I always found time to draw and sketch, and the dream of one day being an artist was always at the back of my mind.

In the meantime, money difficulties increased at home. My father could not manage to make ends meet. I, a fifteen-year-old boy, began to discuss the future with him. We were such a big family, and yet nobody seemed to think it was necessary to sit down and discuss our problems seriously; they just took it for granted that life had to be mean and petty. I was the only one to revolt, the only one who longed for a wider, more fulfilling life.

In the discussions with my father I came to know and admire him more, yet to pity him at the same time. He told me about his youth and how he had come to live in Galatz after having passed his childhood in the northern part of Moldova, in the little town of Falticeni. He too had been in revolt against the narrow, closed Jewish life in the little town and had longed for wider horizons. He had not wanted his education restricted to Talmudic schools but wanted to know more of the big world. He loved music but never had the opportunity to hear it well played or to develop his voice, but he enjoyed singing the synagogue chants and Hassidic melodies.

He was eighteen years old when he married. Wanting to free himself from the atmosphere of "the clan," he took his wife to the big city of Galatz where he thought he would find opportunities of bettering himself. But the children who arrived year after year soon put a stop to his dreams and he became more and more submerged in daily, hard work just to keep the many mouths filled with food. I loved my father very much; he was the most important figure in my life, and his wisdom and sharp mind had always been an inspiration to me. And I then started to feel great pity for this big, handsome man with so many talents, whose dreams had been destroyed by the pressures of daily life. It was I to whom the thought first occurred that perhaps the family should go back to Falticeni, where a great number of our relatives lived, as well as old friends to whom my father was a loved and respected figure.

The discussions about a return to Falticeni took place after a very painful incident: Some children in the Jewish street were playing with a ball which fell into the courtyard of the corner house, the one house in the neighborhood occupied by Rumanian Gentiles. The owner of the house had two sons, officers in the army, who always looked with contempt at the Jewish community. None of the children dared go into the courtyard to reclaim the ball, but my father, always ready to do a kindness, thought that he, with his imposing appearance, could retrieve the ball without trouble. Therefore he rang the bell and entered the garden After a few minutes I saw him returning, his face red and his eyes bright with tears.

"I did not get the ball back," he said, "but the young officer slapped my face just because I came in to ask for it. May God punish them!"

I was only fifteen years of age, a thin, not very strong youngster, and of course no physical match for the man who had insulted my father. But how I longed to be able to punch his nose in return!

In my humiliation I swore that I would not always live in such a country. Maybe it was at that moment that it became clear to me that one day I would go and live in a country where a Jew could lead a free, dignified life—Palestine. But at the time, the thought uppermost in my mind was that we should move back to Falticeni.

My father considered the proposal seriously and before long he went there on a preparatory visit. He returned with high hopes, bringing with him a photograph of his grandmother on his mother's side. She was a very old impressive lady, the matriarch of the whole clan. Being curious to see me, she had given my father the money to pay for my trip to Falticeni. The idea of traveling by train for the first time appealed to me tremendously. I decided to bring my great-grandmother a present; so, in pencil, I copied her portrait from the photograph. My father decided to return to Falticeni to find a house for us, as he expected to get a job there. I was to meet him later, as my railway ticket allowed me to stop off at the big city of Jassy, and I was anxious to see the university and a new art school there.

Carrying my valise, I walked from the railway station up the main street of Jassy. Before going on to Falticeni I was to stay with a relative for a couple of days. Jassy was like another world. It was a lively, bustling city, the capital of the northern district of Moldova, and it was considered the second city of Rumania.

As I walked along I saw a sign, "School of Art," and an announcement that an exhibition of students' work was being held. I did not hesitate for a moment and entered the building, excited at the thought that at last I was in a sanctuary of art. On the walls were mostly charcoal drawings and watercolors, with a few oils, the artistic quality of which I was unable to judge.

But what impressed me were the students, the young people walking from one room to another, talking, discussing, gesticulating, and clearly living and enjoying the type of life they desired, whereas all I had were my dreams. Whether from exhaustion, excitement, or the heat of the rooms, I fainted. The next thing I knew, I was stretched out on a table with people surrounding me and someone rubbing my temples with vinegar. As quickly as I could, I found my valise and escaped from the building, feeling very ashamed of myself.

That was my first encounter with art school life and it filled me with longing and the feeling of what I was missing. I do not recall anything else of my two days in Jassy, except that wandering through the streets I came upon a young man sitting in a backyard before an easel, painting. I walked shyly into the yard and stood by him, not daring to start a conversation but just enjoying watching his brush fill the canvas with color.

Arriving in Falticeni, from the first day it felt like a place I had known before; the little crooked houses and streets and the people who were mainly Jewish seemed to take me to their heart at once and I felt that I should have been born there and not in Galatz. I had a fantastic number of relatives and they treated me as if I were a new feather in their caps, a youngster bringing with him a fresh and different air. I enjoyed being alone with my father, and we quickly found a house outside of town. It had a big yard and barn and I had dreams of a farm with animals.

The family duly arrived from Galatz and the house had to be arranged to accommodate us all. The one thing I wanted was to have a room of my own, but the rest of the family could see no validity in my request. In the

THE MILKMAN 1920 *oil on canvas* 30 × 26
collection of the artist

end I was allowed to have a narrow little corridor near the entrance to the house. I scrounged furniture from my relatives and decorated the walls with my sketches. Although my "room" was small, it had a big door leading to the yard, which contained some old trees. The green, open space and the singing of the birds gave me enormous pleasure.

I continued studying at home with my older brother, Baruch, to whom I was deeply attached. He developed a gift for journalism and from time to time had articles published in different newspapers. For the first time, my father had a job which brought in an income sufficient for our meagre needs, and the burden of continual worry about money matters was lifted.

Our rural surroundings brought quiet to my mind, and more and more the desire awoke in me to enlarge my knowledge and eventually become an artist. I swallowed book after book, anything I could lay hands on, but mainly biographies of men who had made something worthwhile of their lives. My father had thought to provide for his family by keeping a cow, a goat, some chickens, and a horse and wagon to take us to the market, which was some distance from the town.

Each morning my task was to lead the cow and goat out to the meadows and let them roam around. I would stretch myself out in the long grass, reading or just gazing at the passing clouds above my head or at the faraway landscape, where I could see a little lake and a train passing from time to time. The family thought my dreaminess was due to ill health and that I should see a doctor. But then the weather changed; my days of dreaming in the open air were over. I had to spend my time doing odd jobs in the house or taking care of the animals, and reading and drawing when I could find the time.

I began to be a good chess player and that brought me a sort of fame among the town *kibbitzers*, who were already talking in the coffee houses about an unusually talented young chess player. All the while, the idea of Palestine was taking stronger root in my mind and heart. I began to see that the only way to fulfill my longings was to make the journey to Palestine and, free from the restrictions of my home life and surroundings, start a new life and find my way in art.

Occasionally I sent some of my drawings that had escaped being used by my mother for wrapping paper, to my old school friends in Galatz, and thence these found their way to exhibitions held by Zionist groups elsewhere. I tried to find jobs that would bring in a little money and managed to buy myself a bicycle on which I roamed through the countryside, seeing and enjoying the different types of landscapes. I sometimes lost my way and had to be brought home by a villager in his cart. When I look back on these years from fifteen to seventeen, it seems to me that they were passed in a haze of dreaming about going to Palestine, reading books, especially the Bible, and soaking myself in the beauties of nature.

   GIRL WITH POMEGRANATES 1922 *oil on canvas* 33 × 29¼ collection, Mr. Charles Clore, London

My First Portrait in Oils

From this period of my youth prior to my departure for Palestine, there remains clearly in my mind the visit of my grandfather, my mother's father, Rabbi Israel Dayan. He was the rabbi in the little town of Harlau and his visit to us, by horse and wagon, was his first trip outside his own environment. He had heard that Rivile was actually about to make a trip to Palestine and he was greatly excited at the thought that one of his descendants had been chosen by the Almighty to go to the Holy Land and would be able to touch the Western Wall of the destroyed Temple that had once been the glory of Israel. Such an event warranted his leaving his congregation for a little while.

I spent much time with him in quiet talk, listening to his unusual philosophy. I still had with me the remains of the tubes of oil paint that a school friend long ago had stolen from his sister to give me, and I decided to try and paint a portrait of my grandfather. I had no brushes so I used my fingers, and instead of canvas I used a piece of cardboard.

My grandfather had blue, childlike eyes, a beard that was a mixture of fair and white hair, and the gentle withdrawn expression of someone who does not really live in this mundane world. My mother told me that he permitted himself to eat meat only on the Sabbath and otherwise lived on a glass of milk and a roll a day.

My father's father, Haim Dovid, was just the opposite in character. When I came to know him he was already old, and all of his eleven sons and daughters were married and had children of their own. He was a big, solid, hearty man before whom his grown children still trembled, and well do I remember how he used to drink a glass of brandy every morning at breakfast.

The joy I had in painting the portrait of my grandfather, Rabbi Israel Dayan, is still vivid to me, despite all the years that have since passed. How wonderful it was to see his face growing under my fingertips and to realize that I was able to give form and color to what I saw before me. The very feel of the paint was almost intoxicating to me.

My family and the members of my grandfather's congregation were amazed not only at the likeness I had produced but that a rabbi had agreed to sit for his portrait. How had such a thing come about? With his sweet smile my grandfather replied that there was no law either in the Bible or in the Talmud prohibiting a grandfather from giving pleasure to his grandchild. Was not making a child happy surely one of the finest things a man could do? "If you love humanity," he said, "you love your children and want to give them happiness, and this is one of the most important lessons we learn from the school of Hillel in the Talmud."

MY GRANDFATHER 1910 *oil on cardboard* 12 × 10
collection of the artist

A Dream Comes True: I Go to Palestine

Go!
Some one tells me.
And I do not ask who
Gives me an order so.
I rise from the ground,
Fling off the snow.
I take my grandsire's staff in hand
and off and away . . .
I go.

From my early childhood I had dreamed of going to Palestine. It seems to me now that I always knew instinctively that that was the country where I could develop as a "Jewish artist." By "Jewish artist" I don't mean a painter of Jewish subjects, but one whose roots are embedded in the soil of his own homeland, Zion—where the Bible lives naturally for him and where he feels in his rightful place and is spiritually at ease. I could not have been more than six years old when I began to feel and understand the call of the land of the Bible.

Although we were very poor, people liked to come to our house because of its warm and friendly atmosphere, and among our many guests were the *schlichim*, the emissaries from the various Jewish organizations which existed at that time in the Holy Land. They used to come to our house to sleep and eat for a day or two while they made the rounds of the Jewish community; then they would disappear for a couple of years.

I remember one especially. With his beard, his *payot* (side curls), and stained *capote*, he looked no different from the other *schlichim*. But he happened to stay with us over one of the Jewish holidays, and to welcome the feast he went to the communal bathhouse and returned wearing a silk and velvet mantle in brilliant colors, and a shiny *strimel*. Suddenly to my childish eyes he appeared like King Solomon arrayed in all his glory. This was how a king should look!

MY FAMILY 1925 *oil on canvas* 64 × 50½ collection, Tel Aviv Museum, Lord Plumer Prize

My head was full of stories of the Bible and of romantic Jewish books such as *Ahavat Zion* (Love of Zion) and *Zichronot Beit David* (Memories of the House of David), which my father used to read aloud on Friday nights. Soiled and torn, almost every page turned down by the many readers, these books used to be peddled around for a penny a week. It was from my favorite place behind the stove that I used to listen to these stories of a beautiful country full of vineyards and palm trees where King David reigned and where young men and women danced and sang. The family and friends used to sit around my father, drinking in the words and weeping for joys past and my imagination was excited by what I heard.

Then when the *shaliach* appeared in his fine robes, dressed to go to the synagogue, I felt that the stories I had heard were based on actual facts and that somewhere such a beautiful country did exist. In our poor ghetto, where the colors were only grey and black, the *shaliach* seemed like the angel who appeared to Jacob. I was unable to say a word to him. He touched me on my forehead and said that he would give me something. And then from his not too clean handkerchief he took a few figs and some almonds.

"These come from over there, from near the tomb of Rabbi Meir Bal-Ness," he said. "There is no snow or sleet there like here, but always sunshine and song. The almond trees are pink with blossoms and the fields are full of flowers. Over there was written King Solomon's 'Song of Songs.' Now you are only a little boy, but one day you will go there and see it all for yourself. We are poor people and we have to go around begging for our charities. But in our hearts we are rich. One day the Messiah will come and will bring back to us the beauty and joy of the time when the temple stood in Jerusalem."

I doubt whether I understood what was being said to me, but nonetheless it made me feel happy. I was a quiet child who did not play wild games like other children. My heart told me that the dark days would pass and that a time would come when all these dreams would become a reality.

As soon as I learned to read I steeped myself in the stories of the Bible, and I was eager to learn of everything that came from Palestine. I began to hear about a movement called "Zionism" and of Theodor Herzl and his book *Altneuland*. I sought out friends among those who felt as I did and I tried to study the history of the people of which I was a part.

Then, in 1911, when I was seventeen, something unexpected happened. One day I received a letter addressed to me in Falticeni. It contained a photograph and two gold coins, 10-kronen pieces. The letter was from a Dr. Adolph Stand of Vienna. I did not know him, in fact, I had never heard of him, and it was only later that I learned that he was one of the most important figures in Zionism at that time. He wrote that he had seen some drawings of mine at the Zionist Congress in Vienna. He had liked them and wished to buy them for the two gold coins he enclosed. He said, moreover, that he thought I should go to Jerusalem and study art at the Bezalel School. It all seemed very strange to me, a sort of miracle. It was a fact that I was always drawing, but I had no recollection of having sent any of my work to the Zionist Congress. All I could conjecture was that perhaps a friend to whom I had given some drawings had sent them to be exhibited there. However, it had happened. There I was with two gold coins—a fortune! And a letter of encouragement such as I had never expected to receive.

To go to Jerusalem and study to be an artist! So what I had dreamt of as a child was not just fantasy; now it depended on me to realize all these hopes. The letter and its contents created unbelievable excitement in our little quarter. Everyone talked about it with, needless to say, dozens of exaggerations. The number of gold coins I had received from Vienna became greater with each telling. My supposed good fortune was discussed even at the synagogue. It was said that I was going to make millions.

I was afraid to show myself and did not know whether to admit or deny the rumors. I had never been out of Rumania, and Palestine and its art school were beyond my comprehension. My father was a poor, good, unsophisticated man, with a warm heart, many children, and little income. What did he know of the world? As for me, although it seemed impossible of fulfilment, I started to work toward the goal of going to Jerusalem.

Then, a few weeks later, another letter arrived, this time from Jerusalem. Written in Hebrew, it was from the Bezalel Art School and was signed by Professor Boris Schatz, the founder and director of the school. A letter in Hebrew from Jerusalem and sent by post, not brought by a *shaliach* as was usual! Once again the whole quarter talked of it. My father knew Hebrew, so he was the first to read the letter. And there, clearly stated, was the fact that Professor Schatz had seen my drawings exhibited at the Zionist Congress, had talked with Dr. Stand, and both had agreed that I should go to Jerusalem and become a student at Bezalel. My heart glowed. I would become a real painter and would help Professor Schatz to create Jewish art in Palestine! There was no need for me to worry; the Bezalel School would take care of everything.

IMMIGRANTS AT REST   From the Album of Woodcuts, "The Godseekers"   1923   THE DREAMERS

45

TEL AVIV SEASHORE 1920 *oil on canvas* 22 × 23 collection, Mr. and Mrs. A. Polany, Tel Aviv

The letter was read in every meeting place, and continually talked of. Reuven is leaving, tomorrow, the day after tomorrow. Reuven has received money, much money. He is awaited by the greatest man there. Surely this is a sign that the Messiah will come soon. The Jews will dance and sing and, who knows?—maybe the Temple will be rebuilt. The Temple cannot be rebuilt without artists and the artists will learn from the Bible exactly how it should be made glorious and beautiful. Poor Jews with golden dreams . . .

Even if I had preferred to stay in Rumania I would have been forced to go to Palestine, as everybody expected it of me and kept asking when I was leaving. But the fact was, I had no idea how to set about it. I did not know how much money I needed or where to get the ticket for the journey. My friends at the "club," where we discussed Zionism and Hebrew literature, were just as ignorant as I was. From our geography lessons we remembered that our little town was a long way from the port on the Black Sea from which the ships sailed for such places as Constantinople, Port Said, Alexandria—all nothing but names to us. My friends had already given me a farewell party and everybody had wished me good luck. Still I had no idea what to do.

What I did know was that I had to have some more money. I had a bicycle, an old one. I sold this for forty francs and, with the two gold coins I had received, this made up my traveling money. Then I learned that I would need a passport. But how could I get one? I did not even have a birth certificate and my father was not even a Rumanian citizen.

A government employee luckily took pity on me and gave me two certificates to be filled out stating that my father and I had been born in Rumania. With these forms properly completed, I would be able to obtain a *laissez-passer*. My father did not know exactly where he had been born or on what date, and his father could not remember. But it was thought that my father had been born in the village of Bourdijan.

I went to the market place there, where I had been told that there were three peasants who might remember my grandfather and the birth of my father. A glass or two of wine jogged their memories and they offered to affix their thumb marks on a paper which said that my father, Joel, son of Haim Dovid, was born in the village of Bourdijan on such a day of such a month of the year 1848.

Happily, I returned to Falticeni and, following the same method, obtained a paper about my own birth. In due course I was given a *laissez-passer*. So there I was with a "document," and again the quarter had something to talk about, for I was the first Jew there to ever have a *laissez-passer* issued to him.

Some time later I received a letter from a man in Bourdijan who signed himself "Rubin." He wrote that he thought I might be a relative, which was not likely, since my family name was Zelicovici, and not "Rubin". The name Rubin, was my first name, and I used it then to sign my paintings, as I do till this day. He heard I was going to Palestine and asked me to be good enough to take his old grandmother, who had dreamt all her life of dying in the Holy Land. He said that she was eighty-two, had no travel documents and could not make the journey alone. I, a lad of seventeen, full of good will and ideals, answered the man that I would be glad to take the old lady with me and suggested where we should meet.

Nobody knew what a youth needed to take on a voyage to Palestine. My *t'fillin*, of course. Then a bag of dry biscuits baked by my mother, a dozen hard-boiled eggs, olives, salt, pepper, tea, coffee, sugar and also an alcohol lamp on which I could boil water and make a glass of tea. My mother made me a little bag in which to keep my gold coins and the money from the sale of my bicycle. What else could a young man need? Nothing. As soon as I arrived in Jerusalem that wonderful art school would take care of all my needs. Neither my parents nor I doubted this for a moment.

Then the question of taking the train arose. I was advised not to buy a ticket. Why waste the money? You enter the train and sit down. If the guard does not come along, all the better. If he does, then you tell him you are not going anywhere, just taking a little ride. If he is a good man, he will merely nod pleasantly. If he is not, then the other people in the carriage will help you. All this I solemnly believed.

As it happened, I did know the guard on the little train that took me to the station and he did not even bother to ask me for my ticket. At the junction I looked for the old lady whom I had never seen. The train was due to leave and still I could not find her. Then, sitting on a bench near me in a third-class carriage, I noticed an old lady with a bundle. She was telling some people behind her that she was in trouble, as she was going to Palestine and had to meet a relative named Rubin and did not know where he was.

At this point I made myself known to her; she gave me her bundle and told me that God will bless me and help me.

The trip to Constanza takes twenty-four hours with three changes of train, all to be undertaken without a railway ticket or food or drink. But somehow we managed; most of the travelers were Jews, sympathetic toward a young man going to Palestine and ready to be of use to him.

Once arrived at Constanza there was the problem of getting passage on a ship. After many inquiries I found that there was a ship due to leave for Constantinople that very night. A friendly sailor took me to an officer who, after some conversation, learned that I played chess. It seemed that he was a very keen chess player himself, and as he would like a partner on the trip to Constantinople, he was willing to arrange my passage. I was to come back to the ship when darkness fell.

Even when I returned with my "old lady" he made no protest but pushed both of us into the hold of the ship. Then, almost immediately, he wanted to have a game of chess with me. I allowed him to win the first game but the second and third games I took from him. However, he seemed pleased that he had managed to win even one game from such a good player. At midnight the whistle sounded and the ship was off to Constantinople.

The next morning I hurried out of my cubbyhole to have my very first look at the sea. It was an overwhelming experience; I fell in love with the sea at first sight, a passion that I still have. The changing blues, greens, purples, the rhythm of the waves with their ebb and flow: all this fascinated me from the start.

I can still recall my surprise at seeing so many people walking about the deck; I had been naive enough to think that my old lady and myself were the only passengers. I was amazed to see people stretched out on deck chairs, a woolen cover thrown over their legs, and breakfast being served to them.

Walking around the deck, I noticed a tall man with a black beard coming toward me, who resembled the late Dr. Theodor Herzl, whom I had revered. For some reason he stopped to talk to me, perhaps intrigued by my mop of black hair, gaunt face and shabby clothes. He introduced himself as Dr. Kaufmann of Vienna. I told him that I was going to Jerusalem to study art at the Bezalel School.

Becoming excited, he said that he had been to Palestine several times and would be glad to help me. My first problem, I told him, was that of accommodations for the old lady and myself when we arrived at Constantinople. At once he said that he knew of a place near the harbor where we could stay overnight. He no longer seemed to me a mortal Dr. Kaufmann from Vienna, but rather an angel from above.

Sure enough, when the ship docked, Dr. Kaufmann led us through the harbor of Galata to a shop with the sign, "Pharmacy." Through the window it looked like the habitat of a sorcerer: bats, snakes and all sorts of colored remedies in large bottles, and spiders' webs everywhere. The owner looked like a little gnome, with a hooked nose, short, scant, reddish beard and bright eyes that peered at me over his glasses.

After Dr. Kaufmann spoke to him quietly, he told me in Yiddish that the old lady and myself could pass the night in the little room at the back of the shop. The next morning Dr. Kaufmann took me and the old lady, who despite her eighty-two years insisted on coming too, around the city. The port of Galata is connected to Constantinople by a bridge, and I was fascinated by the sight of hundreds of people jostling one another: beggars, street-vendors, porters carrying huge cases. At the entrance to the bridge sat a row of government employees with metal trays tied to their waists into which the users of the bridge had to throw toll money. Another exciting experience was visiting the Sophia market with its noise, color, the constant movement, the crowds and the stalls. I did not know how to thank Dr. Kaufmann for all his kindness, so I made him a little sketch with which he seemed delighted.

Later that day Dr. Kaufmann introduced me to a young man named Dante Alighieri, after the famous poet. He was the secretary of the Italian Opera Company, which had been playing in Constantinople but was leaving the next day for an engagement in Athens. Dr. Kaufmann explained that the old lady and I wished to leave for Palestine, and the charming Italian immediately said that he would include us in his group of thirty-six people, who had a collective ticket. I could travel as a member of the group and the old lady could pose as a dresser. Before taking leave of my kind acquaintance from Vienna, he gave me a letter to a certain Mr. Kamenitz, who was the owner of the largest hotel in Jaffa, asking him to let me have a room on his account.

I no longer remember the name of the ship but only that it took us a couple of days to arrive at Piraeus and that the members of the opera company received us cordially and were very willing to pose for me. Dante Alighieri introduced me to an Italian engineer who was going to Alexandria in connection with a trolley car scheme. He had a very beautiful wife who spoke French. I made several sketches of the couple and they provided my old lady and myself with food and drink.

When we arrived at Alexandria we found out that a boat for Jaffa was leaving from Port Said that very night, and we therefore had to take a train immediately from the harbor. I put my old lady on the train while I hurried off to buy a sandwich. When I returned, what did I see but the old lady holding hands with the beautiful wife of the engineer, while they both wept! It happened that the young woman was the daughter of a Rumanian rabbi. She had left her home because she had fallen in love with the engineer, and her family had no knowledge of her whereabouts. She begged my old lady to pray at the Wailing Wall for her and her family.

We arrived without mishap at Port Said and were informed that a Russian boat taking cattle to Jaffa was in port and would accept passengers. I changed one of my gold coins and bought passage for my old lady and myself. Little did we know what awaited us.

The boat was nothing but a big box with no place to sit down; we all had to stand, holding on to the railing which went around the deck, while in the hold hundreds of cattle stamped, snorted and screamed. To make matters worse, as soon as the boat set sail, a storm blew up. This terrified the cattle, who now bellowed madly, while the sailors tried to calm them. And the passengers, all of whom seemed to be orthodox Jews going to Jerusalem, prayed and moaned all night long. Some of them, however, found an opportunity to question me as to why a young man like myself wanted to go to Palestine. They drew a miserable picture of conditions there. This was surely not an encouraging prelude to my arrival in my dreamland.

But at length the night passed, the sun rose, and the sea became quiet. The orthodox Jews put on their *tallitoth* (prayer shawls) for the morning prayers. Soon Jaffa came in sight, its minarets and flat-roofed houses outlined against a pale blue sky, beautiful enough to make me forget the wretched night. No sooner did the boat cast anchor than Arab boatmen climbed up the ladder, took us in their arms and almost literally threw us down into the little skiffs in which we were rowed ashore.

JERUSALEM FAMILY 1924 *oil on canvas* 36 × 29 collection of the artist

I at once asked to be directed to the Kamenitz Hotel and soon found myself in a pleasant, cool hall with a freshly-washed stone floor and an agreeable landlord scanning my letter of introduction. As for my old lady, it was here that we parted company. She was sent on her way to Jerusalem and I did not see her again for twenty years, when she was 102!

I was too excited to rest, and started to walk through the town. I felt as if I must be dreaming, as, for the first time, I saw camels treading the roads and I drank in the sweet smell of the nearby orange groves. I took off my shoes, hung them on a stick which I carried over my shoulder, and walked barefoot in the sand. Rumania, its drabness, its worries and troubles, disappeared from my mind. I walked on and on dreamily, going toward that place where one day a new Jewish city was to arise and become the Tel Aviv that would be my home.

AT REST 1927 *drawing, India ink on paper* private collection Paris

Arrival in Jerusalem

How can one ever forget being eighteen years old and arriving for the first time in Jerusalem on a beautiful spring day to fulfil a dream? In the little Turkish train that brought me from Jaffa, I had my eyes glued to the window, gazing at the landscape and breathing in the air of Eretz Israel. I could hardly believe that it was I, Rivile, from the little town of Falticeni in the Carpathian mountains of Rumania, who was actually in Palestine, traveling toward the hills of Judea. I was amazed to note that everything looked familiar to me; it seemed as if I knew every rock, every tree, the desert hills. As the train came into Jerusalem I felt I was coming home. But as great as was my excitement and fervor over the landscape and the city of Jerusalem, equally great was my disappointment at finding nobody waiting to meet me.

I went straight from the railway station to the Bezalel School of Art, that had been notified of my arrival. The school was in an imposing stone building on the outskirts of Jerusalem, built on rocks and surrounded by a garden. At that time the nearest built-up area was the Arab cemetery in the Mamillah Road, a walk of about twenty minutes. The Bezalel building stood alone, isolated, a symbol of the Jewish revival.

In the school I could not find anybody who knew about my coming. Professor Schatz, the director of the school, was in America. Although I was exhausted from the trip, I was full of enthusiasm and there was nobody to whom I could communicate my feelings. A couple of Bezalel students did try to help me and took me to a house in the oldest section of Jerusalem, Nachlat Shiva, where I found a little room and was able to have a drink and to rest. The house belonged to the head of the Jerusalem *ghari* drivers, a well-known character who owned some fine Arabian horses and a number of carriages, in which he used to drive tourists around the Holy City.

My little room was over the cistern from which the household drew its water. Water was scarce in Jerusalem at that time and it was the custom to collect rain water in a cistern under the house and to draw it up through a hole in one of the rooms. Naturally I had no privacy. The water also attracted the mosquitoes and I can still remember what a liking they took to me.

I explained my financial situation to the person in charge of Bezalel, but he was not of much help. It was agreed, however, that I be taken on in

OLD JERUSALEM 1925 *oil on canvas* 31 × 39 collection of the artist

the section where ivory souvenirs were made, and there I spent my time carving decorations on gift boxes. Jews from Yemen and the Orient, and many from the Old City of Jerusalem, formed the majority of the craftsmen of Bezalel, which was then a thriving enterprise supplying Palestinian arts and crafts to the foreign market and the tourist trade. In the carpet section alone there must have been a hundred people working.

Although called the "Bezalel Art School," it possessed no fine arts section, and other young people who, like myself, had come to study there were forced to turn to souvenir-making for a living. I was very dissatisfied at the turn things had taken and disliked the mechanical nature of the work I was doing. But I was not despondent, as the whole group was alive with idealism and imbued with a healthy, cheerful spirit. We explored the country around Jerusalem; a moonlit night was always the occasion for a donkey ride to the nearby rural villages of Motza or Ein Karem, delightful in their green leafiness. I used to walk alone on the walls of the Old City or wander through its winding alleyways and colorful *suks* (markets).

My sketchbook was always with me, for the city teemed with models: the old Jews devoutly praying at the Wailing Wall, Bokharan women with their brightly-colored holiday clothes, the graceful Arabs in their long robes, the olive trees with their silver leaves, and the stone buildings which seemed to have captured the sunlight. I lived from day to day without thought of the morrow. From time to time I was invited to have a meal with the kind family with whom I lodged, but mostly fruit and vegetables sufficed for me.

This family was most interesting. The husband came from Russia, the wife from Morocco, resulting in a very complex melange of cultural backgrounds and temperaments. I can clearly recall the arrival of the wife's family after the persecution of Jews in Morocco in 1912. They came to Palestine, a clan of some fifty, headed by an old matriarch. They had travelled through the deserts of Libya and Sinai by camel with their furniture, household equipment and personal goods, a journey which took them about three months. With them they had a chicken coop so that they could have meat for the *Shabbat* meals; one of the grandsons was a ritual slaughterer. The proud cock travelled in a coop to himself.

It was said that the family was wealthy and had brought much gold and money with them. One of the youngest grandchildren had brought his bicycle, his dearest, although much repaired, possession. Another prized item was an alarm clock. Their arrival created a great stir in the neighborhood. A large tent was erected in the yard of the house and there the tribe lived until they finally settled themselves.

At Bezalel, some of the young people from eastern Europe agreed with me that we should demand that art classes be started. I certainly had come to study art and not to spend my time as a craftsman. Our "rebellion" did not have much of a result, but rather served as a good occasion for making jokes, drawing caricatures and declaiming. But nevertheless, a group of us did obtain the use of an old loft where we could have a live model pose for us daily. There were no instructors and whoever wanted to come and draw could do so while the Bezalel administration undertook to pay the models two shillings a day. Months later, when Professor Schatz returned, I introduced myself to him and he vaguely remembered having written me a letter. He promised that everything would be straightened out and told me not to be impatient. In due course, art teachers would be brought over.

But the Bezalel School was far removed from the lively art movements that were animating Paris, for instance. There was a library, but it was the works of Liebermann, Israels, Kolbach and Franz von Stuck that were found in illustrations there. Nothing was known of the Cubist movement, for example, then at its height in Paris. We lived isolated in our little Turkish backwater.

Then fate brought a change into my life. One day when I was working in the Bezalel on a piece of ivory, carving a scene of "Samson and Delilah," a tourist from Germany came over to my table. He picked up my piece of work and complimented me on it. A little while later I was called to the office where I found him talking with one of the managers. The tourist wanted to buy one of the ivory boxes I had carved and obviously paid a good price for it, for later the manager gave me a special tip, a Turkish *mejila* (about a dollar).

Outside the office this man, whose name I no longer recall, asked me in German why I was wasting my time in this workshop. He said that I seemed to have talent and was surprised I did not try to go to Paris and study art.

This was the first time that anybody had mentioned to me that Paris was the place to study art; I had been naive enough to think that I could do so in Jerusalem. The man's compliments and his suggestion of Paris put me into a state of excitement; I felt dizzy. I was ashamed to question him further, but the name "Paris" reverberated in my ears.

When I returned to the atelier I told some of the young artists who used to draw from the model together with me what the tourist had said. A sort of frenzy seized us all; we started to bang on the tables, crying out, "To Paris, to Paris!" But I took the idea seriously and from that moment started to plan how to gain my objective. For in my heart and mind I knew that I was not achieving what I had come to Jerusalem for: the study of art. And I knew that a proper preparation for my life's work was my primary aim.

I realized that the first step must be to return to Rumania to see what money I could raise for my venture. In the same way that I had decided to go to Palestine, that is, almost forced to do so by an inner compulsion, so I decided I must go to Paris.

I went through my poor possessions and found a few things I could sell. Within a couple of weeks from the tourist's visit, and after only one year in Jerusalem, I was making arrangements for my departure. But although

I was leaving Palestine, the spell of ancient Jerusalem was upon me and I knew in my heart that I would be returning. The Holy Land was my ultimate goal, even if the way to it was not as straight as I had at first envisaged.

Poetry had always been a sort of refuge for me, and when I did not feel like expressing myself in line or color it was to words I turned, in my mother tongue of Yiddish. I remember that I wrote poems at this time, one of which, the "Legend of the White City," especially expressed my feelings:

So the young folk pass and perish
In the seven-gated city,
While whoever marked the sand there
He who still might read the message
Does not come.
He does not come.

In Jaffa I bought a deck ticket on a ship carrying emigrant Jews and Arabs to America. I took a ticket as far as Port Said, trusting to luck to help me reach my destination. But when we arrived at Port Said, to my dismay the Egyptian authorities put us all into quarantine for twenty days, as cholera had broken out on the ship. We were all confined in one large room where we slept on the floor. Food consisted of a little rice and *pitta* (Arab flat bread), but some of the group managed to obtain some dates and oranges from hawkers around the building.

Finally the time came when we could continue the trip. But, alas, not me. As I had no money, no passport and no address, I was sent under guard to Alexandria where I was put into prison. Nor was there even a consul to whom I could apply for assistance. I thought I would lose my mind.

The prison guard knew only Arabic and I saw him only when he brought water and *pitta* to my cell window each day. After a week the guard was changed; the new one spoke a few words of French. He allowed me to go out into the courtyard and I stood by the gate determined to try and attract the attention of some passer-by who might help me.

My savior came in the person of a young man wearing a hat with an interpreter's badge on it. When I saw him walking along in the sunshine my hopes rose and I called out to him in all the languages I knew. Miraculously he turned out to be a Rumanian Jew.

My story aroused his sympathy. He generously made a statement to the authorities to the effect that I was a relative of his, and on this basis I was released. I then explained to him that my few possessions had been stolen and all I had was the small bundle with me, whereupon he lent me five francs, saying "I just got you out of prison and already you're asking for money!" But he was a good-hearted person and found me an inexpensive room for fifty cents a day. So there I was in Alexandria with practically nothing in my pocket but at least a roof over my head.

Near my hotel I saw to my joy a sign which read, "Cafe des Artistes." Although this was in the slum quarter of Alexandria, nonetheless the sign gave me some hope, so I went into the cafe with my sketchbook. I saw a number of people sitting at little tables playing cards and I noticed they were all wearing the badge of "Ship's Interpreter."

I sat down in a corner and ordered a cup of coffee, my first in a month, and started to sketch one of the players. He had sideburns and a big mustache and seemed a very lively fellow. The other players glanced at me from time to time and then one of them came over to see what I was doing. He called the others over and they gathered around to look at my sketch or, more accurately, caricature. The man with the mustache asked me what I wanted for it.

"Five francs," I said, having no idea what I should demand. He immediately gave me the money and I handed him the sketch, with my signature. Then several of the other men asked me to do portraits but I made only one more, earning another five francs. The sound of our voices and laughter brought the cafe owner into the room. When he saw me he shouted, "Sara, come here. See who's here!"

He came over and embraced me, saying "Aren't you Yoel Zeltzer's seed? I am Bukanetz from Galatz who used to make your suits. I left Rumania five years ago and am the owner of this cafe."

His wife too seemed overjoyed to see me, although she did not know which of the brothers I was until I told her, "Rivile." I was asked to stay for dinner and to come the next day for lunch. Never was a dinner more welcome, and how I enjoyed the good Rumanian food!

They overwhelmed me with questions, although my talk of studying art in Jerusalem and Paris meant nothing to them. That night I treated myself to a better room at the squalid hotel where I was staying. My next act was to find my benefactor and repay him the five francs he had loaned me. He was very surprised as he had never expected the money to be returned. We became good friends and he advised me to frequent a certain cafe where the wealthier people of the town went and where I could earn money by sketching portraits.

Wearing tarbooshes, smoking narghiles, having shoeshines, playing *sheshbesh* or just talking to one another, the crowd made a motley and fascinating picture. My pencil did not betray me and soon I began adding more five-franc pieces into my pocket. However, I did not want to stay too long in Alexandria; I wanted to be on my way to Rumania.

I located the Rumanian shipping company which had a ship plying from Alexandria to Constanza every two weeks. While I was walking outside the offices of the company, a young man came out and, seeing me, took me by the arm. He proved to be one of my old classmates from the Rumanian High School, named Mueller, whom I had not seen for several years. We started to talk as if we would never stop, and then I thought, I'd better tell him right away that I am trying to return to Rumania. No sooner did Mueller hear what I wanted than he said that he could

SOPHIE 1924 *oil on canvas* 32 × 26 collection, Mr. and Mrs. D. Edgar Cohn, Beverly Hills

HASSIDIC ECSTASY 1923 *oil on canvas* 32 × 26
collection, Mr. and Mrs. Bernard Weinberg, Paris

easily help me, for his uncle was a director of the shipping company. Young Mueller himself was planning to return the following week and offered to take me with him in his first-class cabin.

Thus, in no time at all, my trip was arranged. Providence again was looking after me. There was, however, another problem. How was I going to get from Constanza to Falticeni?

Parting from my old classmate at Constanza, I went straight to the railway station. I was anxious to arrive in Falticeni before *Yom Kippur*, the Day of Atonement, the holiest day of the Jewish year. It would mean so much to my father, indeed to the whole town, if, coming from Jerusalem, I could arrive on time.

The ticket cost thirty-six francs and as all I had left was six francs, I could not pay for it. But I could telegraph my parents to wire me the money. After some time the money did arrive, but it was only thirteen francs. All I could do was to buy a ticket for as far as the thirteen francs would take me.

Carefully carrying the bottle of Palestine wine rolled up in a palm leaf, which I had brought all the way from the Holy Land, I got into the train and looked around for a friendly face. I saw nobody I knew and no one who looked particularly sympathetic. If I got off at an in-between station I would be stranded, so I decided to try my luck. I went into a compartment and lay down on a bench with my face covered with a newspaper, and prayed to God to help me. When the conductor came in and saw someone sleeping, as he thought, he went away. And in this way, undisturbed, I travelled all the way to Falticeni, arriving before the commencement of *Yom Kippur*.

My father was waiting for me and could hardly believe it was really me. "Only to you can such things happen. You go off to Palestine and come back just in time for *Yom Kippur!*" he said.

After greeting all my family, I went to the synagogue for the twenty-four-hour fast. As usual, my father was the cantor and never had his voice sounded more beautiful or more full of feeling. I felt that his prayers went straight to heaven and it seemed to me that the heavens opened to receive them.

In the little town of Falticeni it was the custom to spend the whole night of *Yom Kippur* in the synagogue, praying, telling stories and even sleeping there. The congregation all crowded around me, wanting to hear about Jerusalem. Had I really touched the sacred stones of the Wailing Wall? Were there really vineyards as in ancient times, and did the old men sit in the shade of their fig trees in the noonday sun? These poor Jews, who were not able to earn a decent livelihood and lived in squalor, listened with shining eyes to my stories of a land filled with sunshine, where date palms and fig trees flourished.

I had returned to Rumania in order to be able to go to Paris. The year was 1913 and little did I know what the coming year was to bring.

The Day of Atonement over, I started to investigate how I could

THE DANCERS OF MERON   1926   *oil on canvas*   64 × 50½   collection of the artist

manage my trip. There was the eternal question of money. How could I ask my father, who had so little money with which to support his numerous brood, to furnish funds for me to continue to study? I was torn. On one hand, I felt I should stay in Falticeni and try to earn money to help my father; on the other hand, I felt that the need to paint was the reason for my existence and that it was essential for me to go to Paris. It was not even a question of a conscious desire: an inner urge impelled me to make use of my talent. But in my innocence, I thought that first I should try to make some money for my family, and then I could take leave of them with a lighter heart.

I was fortunate enough to find a job as a bookkeeper in a porcelain factory in the town of Craiova, which was twenty-eight hours by train from where we lived. I was not too badly paid and was able to send half my salary to my family. Whether I was really content or not, I did not know. All I knew was that I must try to leave for Paris as soon as possible. I looked for a quicker way of making money than being a paid employee. Some acquaintances who thought I had a good business sense used their influence to get me into the trade of buying and selling corn. Craiova produced corn and wheat in great abundance. These could be bought fairly cheaply and sold at a good profit in Falticeni where food was scarce, especially during the long and difficult winter months. I managed the affair so well that in a short time I had enough money with which to provide for my family and then leave for France.

My father found it difficult to believe that a young man had been able to make money so quickly in a way he himself had never found possible. He begged me to stay in Rumania a little longer and make some more money; then I could leave with his blessing. Actually he felt that I was a crazy youngster even to want to give up a profitable business for the life of a starving painter. The whole idea of painting as a profession was incomprehensible to him. He felt that what I contemplated doing was akin to committing suicide.

I agreed to stay longer and to make another business attempt. But this time luck was against me. Other people had the same idea as I had and now there were so many competitors in the grain business that not only did I not make any money, but I lost most of what I had gained. I lost also two months of valuable time.

Heartsick, I finally had to tell my parents that they must let me go my own way. The business world was not my world. An inner compulsion forced me toward the life of an artist.

One of my relatives promised that he would obtain a small scholarship for me from the B'nai B'rith organization, and it was on the basis of this promise, of sixty francs monthly for a year, that I made arrangements to leave. It so happened that a group of Jewish actors was going to Lemberg and Vienna and I was able to travel cheaply with them.

It was not an easy decision for me to leave my old parents burdened

MUSICIANS OF SAFED 1937 *oil on canvas* 36 × 29 collection, Lord Sieff of Brimpton

ROAD TO MERON 1923 *oil on canvas* 36 × 36 collection, Mr. and Mrs. Gershom Shocken, Tel Aviv

with a large family and living such poor and difficult lives while I went off to a very unclear future, not knowing what awaited me nor whether I would meet with success or failure. But all the same, I was firmly convinced that my life lay outside Rumania and that Paris was the first step on the way.

In the train I took out my sketchbook, as I always did, and made drawings of what I saw around me, so that I was never bored. In Vienna I had to go from the east station to the west, and I took the opportunity of seeing something of the city.

At last I arrived at Lemberg. The station was in the course of being rebuilt, and, to my surprise, I saw a man on a scaffold, painting a mural decoration. I spent most of the day watching this man handle brush and paint, talking to him and finding out what methods he used. I also asked his advice as to how I could get from Lemberg to Paris as cheaply as possible.

"Simple," he said. "Don't buy a ticket, but put your lugage down in a corridor or compartment. Then, before the train leaves the station, look underneath it for some sort of a support on which you can stretch out. It won't be comfortable and it will be smoky, but you won't be killed, and in this way you'll get to Paris without paying a fare."

As I had no money I followed his advice, and I realized, that if one is young enough, any hardship can be borne. At every station I got out to get some water and something to eat, then returned to the underside of the train. After some time I even had a fellow traveller, a youth like myself, which made the journey less tiresome. I spent three days and three nights in this uncomfortable position, and then at last I was able to stretch my legs and breathe clear air. We had arrived in Paris, at the Gare de l'Est.

SELF–PORTRAIT   1915   *oil on canvas*   21 × 21   collection of the artist

Paris at Last

The first thing I had to do after my arrival was to find an inexpensive place to sleep. I had only about ten francs in my pocket. I soon found a shabby little hotel and although I was tired from the journey I felt I had to go out. How can one rest when one finally arrives in the city of one's aspirations and hopes? Paris. Just to say the name gave me a feeling of exultation.

I started to walk through the streets, not knowing where I was going and not caring. All I knew was that here I was in the art capital of the world, and that I had placed my first step on the road I wanted to take. I don't remember what time I got back to the hotel, but it was in the early hours of the morning.

How beautiful Paris looked in the pale light of dawn! The street cleaners were at work, the carts were bringing huge mounds of vegetables into Les Halles, the milk vans were rattling along. Paris was waking up; I was exhausted. I was hungry. But I can still remember the feeling of joy that filled me. A little cafe had already opened; sawdust was being thrown on the floor. I asked for a cup of coffee and got a bowl of the steaming liquid, accompanied by a soup spoon. I felt that I was already a Parisian and my heart beat heavily with happiness. My worries, my fears, my troubles, all seemed to disappear. I was physically tired but mentally full of energy.

My next step was, of course, to locate an art school. I asked in the office of my little hotel where to find such a school. Nobody had any idea. I was amazed. I had thought that in Paris everybody knew about art and art schools. Then someone suggested that I look through the *Edition Bottin*, which listed all the city's addresses. I sat down to look through the big, heavy volume and at last I found: "Ecole des Beaux Arts, 6, Rue Bonaparte."

What, I thought, could be better than the National Academy of Fine Arts? Taking my sketchbooks with me I made my way to the Rue Bonaparte. When I walked by the portal with the inscription, "*Le dessin est la probité de l'art—Ingres*," I felt a hollow in my chest and a buzzing in my head. I did not know who Ingres was, but the words aroused an echo in me.

I saw a courtyard full of young men walking in all directions, some with canvases under their arms, some with sketchbooks. Some were wearing smocks covered with paint stains. All seemed to be lighthearted and gay. I wondered whether I would ever be like them. How do they manage to live? I asked myself. Where do they get money from? Probably, I thought, they are the sons of rich men or have received scholarships. They seemed to have no troubles.

I found the secretariat and suffered my first disappointment. I was told that I could not be accepted at the Beaux Arts because the examinations had already taken place, but I could prepare myself for next year's tests. I was in despair. Why had I then come to Paris? What would I do for a whole year?

My father was right. I was only a poor Jew from Falticeni and that is where I should have remained. But then, will prevailed over disappointment. I must find a way out. My life meant nothing to me unless I could become an artist. I would have to get into the school without taking the tests, that was all.

I put some more questions to the secretary and soon found out that every professor had the right to admit two or three pupils a year if he considered they had sufficient merit. They were called students "hors concours." Immediately my spirits rose. If others could be admitted hors concours, why not me?

I found a brochure which contained the regulations of the Beaux Arts and also the names of the professors: Bonnat, Colin, Cormon, and others. There were also photographs of the professors. I particularly liked the face of Professor Colin, a typical Frenchman, resembling Napoleon III, with a little beard, a big black hat and a lavallière.

I was informed that if I wanted to see Professor Colin, he lived at 40, Rue Vaugirard. I set off for his house and found that it was enclosed in a garden with a wall to the street and the gate shut. Suddenly I lost my courage. How could I, a little nobody, dare to approach a professor of the Academy of Fine Arts? I walked back and forth and decided that I would wait till he came home for lunch. And soon I saw a man who resembled the professor's photograph, walking toward me with long strides. I accosted him, apologizing for speaking to him, but said that I had come from far away to study art in Paris and because the tests had already taken place, I could not be admitted. I implored him to look at my work as perhaps he would find that I could be admitted hors concours and that that would save me from desperation.

Probably Professor Colin had never heard such wild and pitiful talk from a would-be student. In any event, he told me to come with him to his studio. We entered a big room full of canvases and frames, and then he asked me to show him my work. It was no small sacrifice for a Frenchman to postpone his lunch hour to give time to a person unknown to him, and it was only much later that I fully appreciated Professor Colin's action. As he studied my drawings he grew more and more interested and amused, sometimes laughing aloud at the caricatures. Then he turned to me and said, "You are certainly gifted and I shall be pleased to have you as one of my pupils hors concours."

FLOWERS ON MY WINDOW 1923 *oil on canvas* 29 × 20
collection Tel Aviv Museum, Gift of Mr. and Mrs. David S. Heyman, New York

The trumpets announcing the Messiah's arrival could not have made me happier. Then and there the professor wrote a note to the secretary of the Beaux Arts, announcing his decision. It was a very precious document for me, and I believed that it would be my passport to the future.

Now I had to find a place to live in the students' quarter. I had heard that the Latin Quarter was cheap, so I wended my way there, but to my unsophisticated eye all the apartment houses looked too grand and too expensive. Then I came to the Place de l'Ecole Polytechnique near Montagne Sainte-Genevieve. This quarter looked sufficiently poor to me.

I saw a big building with the pompous name "Grand Hotel des Ecoles," and on a chair by the entrance sat a little old man, the concierge. I went over and told him that I was a foreign art student, newly arrived in Paris. I seemed to have won him over, for he told me that there was a sort of utility room under the stairs, and if I would agree to keep it clean, he would collect some furniture from other rooms and let me have it for eleven francs a month.

The room had a wooden door and two windows which opened onto a yard, but it was fairly large and the noise did not disturb me. Besides, I could not allow myself anything better. I cleaned the room, whitewashed it, and even put up wallpaper. The old concierge was so delighted with my improvements that he brought me not only a bed and wardrobe but also a table, chair, and even a piece of carpet.

"If a young man can make a room look like this," he said, "he does not have to worry. He'll become a great artist."

I gave him five francs on account and felt that now I had a home of my own. In the end I never even had to pay him rent, for he always took a drawing instead and often treated me to a cup of coffee. I became his favorite tenant.

So I had a home but no money. My position was so precarious that I racked my brain for ideas of how to improve the situation. I wondered whether the Rumanian Embassy would give me a loan. This was a very daring idea to enter the head of a poor Jewish boy, but I had no other alternative. The few Rumanian students I knew in Paris were certainly in no position to lend me anything.

I went to the Embassy and asked to see the ambassador. The porter smiled derisively and said that he was not in. Returning to my hotel, I referred to the *Edition Bottin*, which had become my Bible, and noted that the ambassador was Prince Lahovari, a name known to me from history books. The family was of Greek-Rumanian origin and had been leaders of the country before independence.

I returned to the Embassy. Finding a back entrance, I waited there until a car arrived, from which a man in striped trousers jumped out, followed by a secretary carrying a portfolio. I stepped forward and said that I would like to speak to him on an urgent matter. For some unknown reason, the Ambassador did not send me away but took me straight into his private office. As we passed through the outer rooms I could see the surprise

RIDER WITH BOUQUET 1923 *oil on canvas* 32 × 26 collection, Mr. Horace Richter, New York

on the faces of the employees at the sight of Prince Lahavori escorting a thin, shabby young man who certainly looked out of place in an embassy.

I explained my position to the Ambassador and showed him the letter from Professor Colin. I did not ask for charity but for a loan which I promised to repay. Being afraid to ask for too much, I said I would like sixty francs, for I thought this would carry me through the month until I received the money promised by the B'nai B'rith. The Ambassador smiled at the small sum requested but seemed excited about Professor Colin's letter and pleased that a young Rumanian should be accepted *hors concours*.

He took me into another room where he showed the letter to an official, saying, "Who says Rumanian youngsters don't want to study? Please give this young man a loan of sixty francs."

I left the Embassy on air. What more did I need? I had sixty francs in my pocket, a roof over my head, and I had been admitted to the National Academy of Fine Arts! I registered at the school and received a card which carried my photograph and stated that I was a student at the Beaux Arts and therefore entitled a free admission to all museums.

I knew nothing of Paris; my only friend was the concierge of my poor hotel, but I felt full of confidence. The concierge was indeed proud of me and went around the quarter boasting of "my artist who got into the Beaux Arts *hors concours*."

I entered the Beaux Arts, holding my breath as if in a place of worship. I saw a lot of young people walking rapidly back and forth. I knew there were many studios on another floor, but being shy about asking questions, I opened the first door I came to and found myself in a big hall full of casts of statues by Michelangelo. I sat down on a bench, took out my notebook and said to myself, "I have enough work for a lifetime, just copying these sculptures." Those wonderful bodies modeled by a master hand were inspiring even in plaster copies. I discovered the "David" and the "Moses," and echoes from the Bible filled my mind.

I did not even think of looking for the atelier of Professor Colin or finding out what the work program was. The only problem that concerned me was that I should have sufficient paper and charcoal so that I could continue drawing. I came to the Michelangelo hall every day and sat there drawing furiously, my whole being absorbed. I used to go to the banks of the Seine to eat a sandwich for lunch and then back to the Beaux Arts for more drawing and sketching.

I do not recall experiencing any greater emotion than when I first set foot in the Louvre. It seemed to me that I had discovered the very heart of Paris. I walked from one gallery to another. I did not know what to look at first. There were so many artists whose names I had not even heard of! I spent hours just wandering around. I felt dazed and could not even begin to absorb what I saw.

PORTRAIT OF THE POET, URI ZVI GRINBERG 1925 *oil on canvas* 25½ × 21 collection, Tel Aviv Museum

LES FIANCEES 1929 *oil on canvas* 39 × 32 collection of the artist

OLD JAFFA HARBOR 1928 *oil on canvas* 26 × 32 collection, Mr. and Mrs. David Rubin, Tel Aviv

I thought, what a wonderful life I would have in Paris, drawing from the Michelangelo casts at the Beaux Arts and spending the rest of the day feasting on the splendors of the Louvre. My old life in Galatz, in Falticeni, the squalor and mud of the Jewish street—all seemed like a dream of long ago. My real life had now begun here; and yet this too was but a preparation for my return to Jerusalem.

I visited the Louvre every day. I did not yet grasp what it was that constituted the real value of a painting or the greatness of a Rembrandt, a Leonardo or a Fra Angelico. I only knew that I could sit in front of these canvases for hours and that they filled my soul with awe as well as with joy. I longed to have a friend with whom I could exchange impressions. There was so much to see, so much to satisfy my soul, yet nobody with whom to share the feelings and yearnings that had been aroused in me.

Some of the students had apparently noticed the young man who sat alone in the Michelangelo room, drawing, and a few stopped to look at what I was doing.

Nobody spoke to me. Then I noticed that other students had also begun to draw the figures; perhaps they were emulating my example.

One day, one of these young people started a conversation with me. I was delighted to have someone to talk to at last. He invited me to join him for a meal, and as we walked out into the street he said he was going to take me to a place where we could have a good lunch free of charge.

I no longer remember his name; but he was a Bulgarian and at the time seemed like an angel from heaven. My funds had dwindled to almost zero. The place we went to, near the Halles, had been established by a women's society to fight alcoholism. Anybody who showed signs of alcoholism could come in and obtain a free meal together with a bottle of milk. Medical research had established that milk was an antidote to alcohol, and the society's members believed that by providing a free meal and a bottle of milk they were helping to stamp out alcoholism.

My new friend told me that he could not do without alcohol but since he thoroughly disliked milk, I would be doing him a favor by drinking his portion. As a matter of fact I did not drink alcoholic beverages and I actually enjoyed a glass of milk with or without a meal.

When we arrived at the restaurant, the doctor on duty looked at me briefly. He immediately classified me as "alcoholic born of alcoholic parents" (my poor and dearly loved parents had of course been the souls of sobriety!) but I was very happy to receive an admittance card, knowing that I would be assured of at least one nourishing meal a day.

My friend was in his second year at the Beaux Arts and was able to show me through the entire school. In one hall there was an exhibition of the works of contestants for that year's Prix de Rome, while in another hung the paintings of former Prix de Rome winners.

The subject chosen by the contest committee was "La Passion de la Vierge." I think that the work of some twelve candidates was on view and although at that time I was no judge of painting, still I realized that the pictures shown did not represent genuine creativity.

They had been executed according to academic and anatomical guidelines. On one canvas there was a Madonna in blue holding a yellow Christ child, and on another, a Madonna in purple holding a green Christ child, and so on.

I found the exhibition depressing but kept my opinion to myself. The work programs of the various classes were also displayed. I saw that my Professor Colin gave classes with nudes, still life and landscapes. On Monday he taught composition, on Tuesday, perspective; and every two weeks there was a competition among his students.

But at that time I was far more interested in studying the old masters in the Louvre and reading about their lives than in keeping to a set schedule of instructions. As for the art that was being created around me, I knew nothing of it.

Although I was twenty, I was naive, unsophisticated, and poor; and the life of the cafes where the artists congregated was not for me.

At this time both Montparnasse and Montmartre were flourishing. The paintings of Cezanne had been shown; the Impressionists were accepted. Cubism was at its height with Picasso, Braque, Juan Gris as its masters. Young artists from Russia, Germany, Poland, Scandinavia flocked to Paris, attracted by its glitter of new ideas and its artistic ferment.

The academic Beaux Arts was not for them; they had other, more exciting projects in mind. They lived in groups, met daily in the cafes and restaurants for heated discussions on modern art and its future. This I became aware of later. But at the time, I was living in an enclosed world and knew nothing of the artistic revolution that was taking place.

My days stretched between the Ecole de Beaux Arts and the Louvre. It was a lonely life. As I wandered around the Paris streets in the evening I would see young couples on the banks of the Seine, embracing under the trees of the Tuileries gardens.

But I walked alone, wondering how was I going to make my way in life. My Bulgarian friend whom I saw almost daily at the "alcoholics' restaurant" told me that one had to know how to live in Paris. It was not difficult, he said, to find a girl friend who would work for you, a *midinette*, a waitress or a girl working in a factory. Such girls are happy to have a young lover; they ask for nothing and are prepared to do everything they can for him. They are mostly kind-hearted and lovely, he said.

But brought up as I had been in the Jewish Street, dominated by its synagogues, and with morals that had been instilled into me from early childhood, I found his advice repugnant. In my heart I felt that it was bad enough I left home and ate food that was not ritually prepared. These were sacrifices that my art demanded of me, but the idea that my friend put forth was anathema to me.

So I continued my lonely life. I often spent Sundays in the park, listening to a band and enjoying the antics of the musicians rather than the popular music. I never thought of going to the theatre or opera since

I had no money.

In my old hotel there was a restaurant run by a Russian Jewish refugee whose three daughters worked in the kitchen and waited on table. Many Russian and Rumanian students came to eat there. I used to keep the window of my room open so that I could smell the appetizing odors wafted up from the kitchen. I had made some pencil sketches of the three girls and these so pleased the family that in return for the portraits they provided me with Friday night suppers. I felt my lot was quite bearable and that I could manage to carry on, although the stipend payments promised by the B'nai B'rith Society arrived only once. I supposed that they thought I had conquered Paris and was in no need of help.

One day in a street of the Latin Quarter I met an old acquaintance from Galatz. He recognized me first and recalled our days together in the Rumanian High School. He was in Paris to complete his medical studies. Perhaps because of his profession, he noticed my unhealthy appearance and asked how I was managing, and whether I had enough to eat.

I told him that I felt well and was studying at the Beaux Arts where I had been accepted "*hors concours.*" He was very friendly and invited me to come to Meudon where he had a room in a small pension surrounded by trees and grass.

While we were there he took me to see the house of Rodin, the great sculptor, who lived nearby, and who was already a world-esteemed figure. We had the good luck to see him in his garden, a heavy man with a big beard who seemed like a savage god. My friend greeted him and introduced me. I felt privileged to shake his enormous hand and was flattered when Rodin brought out glasses of beer for us. It was the first time I tasted beer and I was afraid to say I did not like it.

In Paris the weeks passed in a regular routine of work, and as the art school secretary observed, I was the first to arrive and the last to leave. As for Professor Colin, I never saw him. Then, one morning, he came into the sculpture room followed by a number of students. Suddenly he recognized me and said, "Is this where you are? I thought you had decided not to come to school. Why don't you come to my atelier?"

I did not know what to reply, and felt awkward. But Professor Colin came over to look at my drawings and said in a loud voice to his assistant, Professor Roche, "He has talent, this young Rumanian. I think I shall recommend him as a candidate from my atelier for the next Prix de Rome."

Some time later I was called to the school secretariat and informed that Professor Colin had indeed recommended me. The news left me in a daze; it was more than I ever hoped for. After reading the regulations governing the award, I saw that first I had to deposit seventy francs with the secretariat to cover the payment for a man who would clean the studio I would be given to work in.

Where would I obtain the necessary seventy francs? How could I compete for the Prix de Rome when I had never used oil paint?

I felt like an impostor. Professor Colin did not know that I had no previous art training and had never used oil paint. Was it possible for an untrained painter to complete for the Prix de Rome? Obviously I had to obtain paints and try my hand at oils.

I managed to raise a few francs to purchase oil paints and canvas, but since I could not afford a model, my subject had to be my own self. The self-portrait I eventually produced certainly owed much to Delacroix, whose paintings I had studied carefully in the Louvre. I myself could not judge the quality of my work and I did not dare show it to Professor Colin, but my friends urged me to submit it to the Salon des Artistes Francais.

Much to my surprise, it was accepted for exhibition and I received a card with *Exposant* written on it.

On opening day I looked everywhere for my painting and at last found it hanging high in a dark corner. But still, there it was, my first real oil painting, and it was on exhibition. I stood in front of it, admiring it for a long time.

One good result of having the painting exhibited was that it brought me commissions for portrait sketches, and in a short while I had accumulated more than seventy francs. I was afraid I might spend the money so I put it into a savings bank of the post office, until I needed it.

So there I was, already a painter who exhibited at the Salon, had seventy francs in a savings bank, was preparing to be a candidate for the Prix de Rome from the class of Professor Colin who had never given me even one single lesson!

I went again and again to see my picture in the Salon. I wanted to hear what people said about my work, and I was not upset when hardly anyone came to the dark corner where my painting hung.

My one true admirer was my concierge; he was most excited about my work being shown at the Salon and boasted about it in the whole neighborhood. Once I took him with me to the exhibition. He put on his Sunday best and I introduced him as my father so that no entrance fee had to be paid. Whether the general exhibition made any impression on him I did not know, but he made a point of tendering me his "official congratulations."

After I had been living at the hotel for some months, the concierge started to sell some of my drawings in order to earn some francs for me. His clients were simple people of the quarter who did not mind parting with a few francs in order to possess "original art." Their attitude was typical of the traditional French respect for art and things of the mind. I was really touched by these sales as I would not have believed that simple, hard-working people, artistically quite uneducated, would part with some of their earnings for the sake of a sketch or a drawing.

I now began to feel more at home in Paris and started to step out of my own part of the city to see what was happening in Montparnasse and in some of the commercial galleries. One day I made friends with another art student whom I used to see in the Michelangelo hall. He was

PORTRAIT OF AHAD HA'AM 1926 *oil on canvas* 64 × 50½ collection, Tel Aviv University

in his second year. His name was Jean Fosse Calderon and he came from Chile. A charming young man, he tried to make me feel less of a stranger in Paris. I remember having breakfast with him one morning in his pleasant little hotel on the Rue de Seine. He opened the door to one room and then passed into a second and still I saw no bed. I could not understand it and asked him where he slept. He said that he had a third room, a bedroom. This was too much for me and I said, "Are you living with your family?"

"No," he answered.

"Then whatever do you need three rooms for?" With my poverty-stricken background I could not grasp the fact that a single person would occupy three rooms. Then I opened a closet door and saw perhaps twenty pairs of shoes. "Why so many shoes?"

"For different occasions," he replied.

All my life I had possessed only the single pair of shoes I was wearing, and if they needed mending I had to wait while the shoemaker repaired them. When I think back I can see that such small, insignificant experiences made a great impression on me and made me realize the narrowness and restrictions of my daily life, although I had already passed my teens and was living in Paris. Inwardly, I still seemed to be the poor boy from the Jewish street in Galatz.

It was Calderon who took me on my first visit to a big Paris gallery, where there was an exhibition of sculptures by Maillol and paintings by Matisse. I had not known that works of this sort existed. I was not only fascinated but possessed by a feeling of exhilaration. I remember very well a painting by Matisse of a woman in a hat. I thought how beautiful it was, how daring, how free. There was a nude by Maillol, "Pomona," which I found wonderful: a rounded woman with heavy legs. How all-encompassing art is, I thought to myself. And this is the field I have chosen. I felt that my life opened before me and if only I could earn enough money to hold myself together physically, then there was nothing that could stop my going ahead.

Although I did not see or hear from Calderon after I left Paris, I shall always be grateful to him for his introduction to the art of our time, which opened my eyes. Only a year ago, I heard from an acquaintance that Calderon had become famous in Chile and only recently had died.

The Beaux Arts closed at the end of June and on the recommendation of some of my fellow students I enrolled at the private Academie Collarossi and arranged to sketch at the Grand Chaumiere. My work at these schools and my drawings from the live model gave me the feeling that I was advancing in my artistic development. Although I never dared approach any of the well-known artists who used to drop into the Grande Chaumiere from time to time, yet seeing them sitting and sketching among the young Bohemian students gave me the feeling that I was starting to learn what Paris really signified to an artist. I let my hair grow long and walked through the streets with more assurance.

June and July were wonderful months. I did not even want to leave the city because of the heat as did so many people, but felt as they left for the sea or countryside that Paris became more and more *my* city. Days I spent at the art schools and the evenings were passed mostly in libraries or in feasting my eyes on the city by night.

Quatorze Juillet

I can still remember the excitement, vitality, movement, and the noise of that day—the dancing in the streets, the fireworks, the unbridled gaiety. The previous day I had helped decorate our square and it seemed to me that at last I was really part of the city.

My concierge told me that every year a performance of grand opera was given free to celebrate the holiday. Of course it meant queueing up to obtain a seat. So a full night before the opera, which happened to be *Samson and Delilah*, I went with one of my neighbors to the Place de l'Opera, which by the time we arrived was already crowded with what seemed to be thousands of people, armed with blankets and food baskets and prepared for a night's vigil.

On the evening of the performance the atmosphere was tense and expectant. The opera was to start at 8:00 p.m., but the gates were opened at 6:00 and the rush began. It was a case of first come, first served. No seats were reserved. I managed to get in before the police closed the gates, but there did not seem to be a single empty seat whether in stalls, grand tier, balcony or up in the "Gods." I even thought I would have to leave. But then I opened a door and found myself in an empty loge. I saw it was the President's loge, which nobody had dared enter. I sat down, however, and a few moments later was joined by some others. A feeling of incredulous delight filled me. There I was sitting in the best part of the house, waiting to hear an opera for the first time in my life and, moreover, an opera with some of the great singers of the world and with wonderful sets and costumes. I put my hand into my pocket to take out the bread and cheese I had brought with me. It was all mashed up so I had to go hungry. But there was the compensation that I was actually listening to grand opera.

The thought was always in the back of my mind that in September I would have to return to the Beaux Arts and prepare for the Prix de Rome competition. At least I had the seventy francs necessary for *"monter un loge,"* and this gave me a feeling of confidence. As usual, I continued to eat my lunches in the "alcoholics' restaurant," in the rue Ticquetonne and made do with coffee and fruit for the rest of my meals.

But storm clouds were gathering in the skies of Europe. Jaures was assassinated. Every day there were demonstrations and manifestations in the streets. Paris became filled with an atmosphere of foreboding and insecurity. I began to find it unpleasant to walk through the streets. My appearance was strange and exotic; people turned to stare at me. Many times, in that year of 1914, I was stopped and questioned about being a foreigner. Who knew, maybe I was a spy!

Overleaf: ARAB CAFE IN JAFFA 1923 *oil on canvas* 35 × 47 collection of the artist

One day a woman came up to me and actually pulled at my long, black hair as if she thought I were trying to disguise myself by wearing a wig. People started to gather around, but when it became clear that it was my own hair, the threatening gestures were lost in laughter and good feeling prevailed.

But I started to sense that my situation was becoming precarious. It was difficult to believe that only two weeks or so previously I had been enjoying a gay *Quatorze Juillet*. Suddenly the pleasant world had become full of darkness and lack of trust. The future looked black. And then came the terrible day of the 2nd of August, with the announcement that war had been declared. Suddenly it seemed as if everybody was on the move; the whole of Paris seemed to be in a state of flux. More and more uniforms made their appearance; I began to feel that I was the only young man walking about in civilian clothes.

At the same time, all sorts of establishments started to close, the "alcoholics' restaurant" in the Rue Ticquetonne being one of the first. Then the Beaux Arts, the Collarossi and Grande Chaumiere Academies closed their doors as did the libraries where I used to read. Paris was no longer the "city of lights," it was dark and mournful. I feared that the authorities would intern all foreigners in the city. My mind turned to the Rumanian Ambassador, who had helped me before, and I felt I should go to the Embassy and find out about my position. I recalled an incident in the Rue Ticquetonne restaurant to which I had paid no attention at the time: a fight broke out between some Balkan students and in the heat of the scrimmage some of them started to shout, "We'll put the whole of Europe on fire with revolution if Montenegro is not freed from Austrian rule."

When I read in the papers about the assassination of Franz Ferdinand and his wife Sophie at Sarajevo, with pictures of the murderers, the scene in the restaurant returned to me. I imagined that I had seen the assassins taking their meals at my poor restaurant.

When I went to the Rumanian Embassy I found it crowded with people. Officials were sitting at a long table calling out various names, mine among them. I was given an envelope which at first I thought might contain a letter from home. But it proved to contain fifty francs and some travel tickets which covered the train journey to Marseilles and a freighter to Rumania. Ambassador Lavohari had also enclosed a few kind words.

I was overcome with gratitude to the Ambassador, a real aristocrat, who in the midst of all his duties, had not forgotten the poor art student who had dared once to approach him. I also learned that the Embassy was opening a free kitchen for stranded Rumanian students, and for about four weeks I lived a haphazard sort of life, making use of the Embassy's kitchen and waiting for the foreigners' evacuation notice. At last, at the end of September, notices appeared announcing that certain trains going south from the Gare du Lyon were at the disposition of the evacuees. I made my farewells to my old friend the concierge, and to Paris itself, as well as

PORTRAIT OF SUZY   1928   *oil on canvas*   32 ×·26   collection, Mrs. Harold Otto, New York to any hopes I might have had for the Prix de Rome. What could the future bring me?

At the Gare du Lyon it looked as if riots had broken out. There was a mob of pushing, screaming people trying to get into the waiting trains, which filled up in no time. I finally managed to squeeze myself in and I recollect that I stood for the greater part of the journey and that rain poured in through the broken windows. When the train stopped at a station I did not even try to get off to buy a sandwich or drink as I feared I would not be able to get on again. After about three hideous days and nights, passed in great discomfort, we finally arrived at Marseilles.

I went to a shipping company immediately and learned that a ship was leaving for Constanza the following day. It was a coal freighter and would probably be the last boat allowed through the Bosphorus, as it was certain that Turkey would also enter the war. The passengers took whatever berths were available, happy merely to sail. In one day we were all black from the coal dust and looked like denizens of an inferno. But we were on the move, and that was what mattered.

Every day we were served a pot of macaroni, a bottle of wine and tea. The ship stopped at various ports but nobody was allowed off; people on the docks looked at us with our black faces as if we were lepers. We were worried that perhaps the Bosphorus would already be closed. Stopping at Constantinople where the ship had to refuel for the rest of the journey to Constanza, we were received with a barrage of watermelons. The Turks looked upon us as enemies, but as long as they threw only watermelons, it did not matter. In fact, some of the watermelons proved good eating. The ship sailed immediately and before long we were at Constanza.

FLUTE PLAYER 1967 *drawing, pen and ink* private collection, Geneva

Trials and Tribulations in Europe

Finally reaching Falticeni, I found my family still living their mean, poverty-stricken lives, content with their mundane chores and never yearning for a more expansive existence. Quickly memories of Paris and my dreams of art sank into the background. I tried to find a corner for myself where I could have my bed, my drawings, and my paints, and where I could find a refuge from their tribal life.

At this time Falticeni was providing asylum for a number of Jewish intellectuals who had escaped from Russia and Bessarabia, They formed an interesting group and I hastened to become one of them, even renting a special room where we used to meet almost daily for discussions and which I also used as a studio. Without their intellectual stimulus I would have been utterly despondent.

As usual, I drew and sketched constantly, finding my subjects in the townspeople. I especially remember the chimney sweep who agreed to pose in exchange for a couple of glasses of brandy, while another model was a gypsy guitar player, one of the town's "characters." One day I read in the newspaper that a general exhibition of art was to take place in Bucharest, at the official "Salon." I sent in the two paintings I had done and, to my great satisfaction, they were accepted. When the organizers asked me to put a price on them, I estimated how much time they had taken to paint and decided that 200 Lei (about $ 40) for each canvas was quite sufficient.

But fate was against me: a fire broke out in the exhibition hall and my works were destroyed. In any case, I had little confidence in my ability to produce a good painting at that time; I felt I was not mature enough, although the self-portrait which I painted at that time, and which I still possess, is not an uncreditable effort.

My general mood though was one of despair and hopelessness. I poured out my feelings in poetry, for which I found a very sympathetic audience in the group of intellectuals to whom poetry and literature were much more meaningful than painting.

At times I even felt that painting was perhaps not the right career for me, and during one of those periods of doubt I first tried my hand at sculpture. Although I had seen a considerable amount of sculpture, both carved and modeled, in Paris, I knew nothing of the craft. All I knew was that plaster hardens when put into water. I thought I would form it into

JAFFA FISHERMAN FAMILY   1927   *oil on canvas*   32 × 26   collection, Mr. and Mrs. David Lloyd Kreeger, Washington, D.C.

a block and then carve out the forms with a knife. I made various experiments, all of which failed due to my lack of technical knowledge. There was nobody to whom I could turn for advice and I remember the day when I simply took the plaster and my sculptural experiments and threw them all away.

I felt that I was wasting my life. Only three years before, I had leaped into the unknown, with my journey to Palestine and then later to Paris. And here I was, back where I had started, a prisoner of a war that I felt had nothing to do with me and which was slowly draining away my youth.

My family was still sunk in their mental apathy and living their poor, circumscribed lives. My father still had the same small job, finding his happiness in the Sabbath and in the Jewish holidays, and in singing in the synagogue. I think he loved me more than the other children and wanted badly to help me in my struggles but he did not know how. He felt I was groping for a broader life but he did not really understand what I was after. He felt guilty at having a son to whom he could bring no comfort or peace of mind. He pitied me and I pitied him as I saw that not being able to help me caused him real suffering.

I looked for work so as not to be an extra burden on him and I found a job in a leather factory, a sort of rather primitive tannery, which belonged to one of my many uncles. I put my whole heart into the work, as I always do with whatever I undertake, and in a short time I made myself useful not only in the office but also in the practical work of the tannery. I watched and listened to the experienced workers and learned from them.

The situation in Rumania was becoming increasingly difficult. Raw materials of all sorts were in short supply, including the chemicals needed for tanning the hides. My uncle went on a buying mission to Italy and took me with him as a so-called "expert." Our destination was the port of Genoa to which the chemicals, imported from the Argentine, were consigned. I was very excited about the trip although I did not know how we would manage, for I was certainly not a businessman, while my uncle knew no languages other than Rumanian and Yiddish. However, making use of my French I did manage to get in touch with the people my uncle wanted to see. It was a boring and unsatisfactory period for me, talking with agents, writing business letters. I was happy when my uncle sent me to Rome to try to obtain government approval for the export of the chemicals and to engage a lawyer to look after the legal aspects of our affairs.

Italy was not yet at war but I can clearly remember a scene in the Quarto dei Mille (near Genoa) where there was an outdoor demonstration at which D'Annunzio spat fire at the Austrians. I was sure that Italy would enter the war soon. My uncle returned to Rumania, instructing me to finish the formalities in Rome, which meant an additional stay of two or three weeks. I began to visit all the museums and to drink in the beauties and glories of that city. I blessed the leather business which had given me

this unique opportunity to study closely the great Italian artists. When the actual deal was long finished, I still remained in Rome, fascinated by the Italian people and their way of life, the stimulation and warmth that one felt in the very air. But, as usual, money was getting very short. There was no more income from the business and I was allowing myself to drift along.

I made a few caricatures for some newspapers, which were exhibited in the windows of the Via Nationale. The *Corriere de la Sera* asked me whether I would be prepared to go to the front as an artist when Italy would enter the war, but that always was a possibility for the future. For the moment, I managed to exist on one meal a day and time sped by without too much worry. Italy was certainly preferable to Falticeni and although I was living aimlessly, it was under a blue sky and among museums and beautiful surroundings.

But one of the caricatures I had managed to sell, with Hindenberg as the subject, got me into trouble and resulted in my having to leave Italy. Italy was already at war with Austria but not yet with Germany, and the police informed me, although very politely, that such a caricature was not permissible and that my presence in Italy was not desirable. A policeman accompanied me to Como to see that I really left the country and I was put across the Swiss border. Thus ended my wonderful sojourn in Italy.

Once in Switzerland, I realized that what I had to do was try and return to Rumania. The difficulty was in being able to arrange it since I had very little money; and going through Austria to Rumania was bound to be difficult, for talk about pending war between the two countries was already in the air.

In the meantime, as always, my eyes were open to anything taking place in the art world. I saw an announcement in a newspaper of a big exhibition in Zurich of the work of Ferdinand Hodler, the most important Swiss painter of that time. I immediately decided to see it. To my dismay, when I arrived at the doors of the Zurich Museum I found that the show had just closed. Dejectedly, I sat on the museum's steps, when I observed a man approaching whom I recognized from photographs as the painter, Hodler. I told him I had just arrived from Italy and was leaving Switzerland shortly and the one thing I wanted to see, this exhibition, I would have to miss.

He smiled kindly and said that although the paintings had been taken down they were still in the gallery, and if I came in with him he would show them to me. So there I sat for an hour or so together with the great Swiss master, carefully looking at one canvas after another.

I was greatly impressed by the strength of his drawing and the monumentality of his compositions—the figures against a typical Swiss background with folkloristic elements. His landscapes proper did not attract me so much.

Hodler was very friendly and straightforward and explained to me something of the way in which he set about organizing his canvases and I listened to him carefully. Undoubtedly Hodler and his work were to have some influence on my own development. I blessed the Italian police for sending me out of their country and into Switzerland.

The question of getting back to Rumania arose again. Sitting in a cafe near the Italian border, I wrote a card to a friend in Rome asking his advice. In my innocence, I thought that since I was so close to the border my card would arrive sooner if I posted it from the Italian side. An Italian letter box was not far off, and so without much thought I made for it, not realizing that by so doing I was illegally crossing the border.

As I was returning, a Swiss policeman approached me and asked me what I had thrown into the Italian letter box. He did not believe my simple explanation but took me to the police station where I was searched thoroughly; even my shoes were subjected to the minutest scrutiny. After being kept at the police station all day, it was finally decided that the best thing to do with me was to send me out of Switzerland, straight to Austria. A policeman took me to the border town of Buchs and told me to take a train to Innsbruck, thence to Vienna and thence back to Rumania.

I felt quite helpless, being handed over from one policeman to another. The realities and formalities of state frontiers and political boundaries had no meaning for me, and were totally beyond my comprehension. While I was waiting for my train at Innsbruck I was again suddenly accosted by a policeman. Austria was at war, so it was normal to be suspicious of a wild-looking foreigner. He asked for my passport, looked at it, saw no stamp of entry and said that he would have to put me on the first train that went back to Buchs. There happened to be a train full of Swiss students returning home after a winter sports competition at Innsbruck, so I became part of their group and had no difficulty getting into Switzerland. Together with them I went to a beer house and passed a cheerful night. One of the group must have given me his room, and when I came downstairs the following morning, the owner of the place told me I could not remain any longer, because I had no legal entry into Switzerland and he was afraid of trouble.

So, off to the railway station again, but this time the train went straight to Budapest. When I arrived at the Budapest station I was told that nearby was a café renowned for its chess players from all over the continent who used to meet and play there. Perhaps I would find some enthusiasts there and some much-needed luck too.

I found the café without much trouble. There were a number of elderly men playing chess as if there were no war on. Going over to one of the tables, I played the typical "kibbitzer's" role, giving unwanted advice. I was anxious to be asked to join a game and eventually one man did ask me to play with him. Putting my whole mind to the matter, I won the first game, and then the second.

My opponent then got to his feet and introduced himself as "Baron von. . . ." The name did not convey anything much to me, but the man's demeanor was that of an important personality. He asked me a number of questions about myself and then suggested I have a meal with him.

I told him my story briefly and let him know that I was stranded and without money. He was obviously a very kind person and, touched by my story, arranged for me to have a room at his hotel. He even provided me with a ticket to the Rumanian frontier in Transylvania. Once again, the unexpected kindness of a total stranger set me on my way.

After an uneventful journey I arrived in the little town of Brasow in the Transylvanian mountains. It was winter weather, cold and snowy. How was I going to be able to make the rest of the journey home to Rumania? The problem of where to stay while in Brasow was solved by a kind Jewish family who took me into their home. Since I was an "illegal visitor" I seldom went out, in order to avoid being spotted by the police, and used most of my time trying to plan how to get over the border. I spent no less than eight days with this family in their pleasant home filled with young sons and daughters. They were interested in hearing all I could tell them about life in Palestine and about the life of an art student in Paris. They were naive, provincial people, but with kind hearts and even if I have forgotten their names I still recall their friendliness with much gratitude.

One day they told me that they had found someone who would lead me over the border by way of a snow track which was not being watched. They gave me food and some money, and after walking in the snow for over four hours, I found myself near the railway station on the Rumanian side of the border.

Again home in Falticeni, I was soon back at my old job in the leather factory and steeped once more in the same dull, depressing atmosphere. My only escape from falling into mental inertia was in writing poetry, some of which was read by a few friends in the "club" but most of which was simply thrown away. I never thought that any of these outpourings would see the light of print.

The end of 1915 and the beginning of 1916 saw me in a mood of black despair. The world was in flames—true, Rumania was not yet at war, but was expected to enter any day—and I myself was without any hope that the purpose of my life, painting, could ever be fulfilled. Also there was no one near me sympathetic with my longings.

My only satisfaction was the natural beauty that the spring weather brought to our town. Falticeni was surrounded by orchards of plum, apple and pear trees, and the blossoms were a joy to behold. I remember that I did not do much work at the factory but sped away to the fields whenever I could.

I decided that I must learn French thoroughly and acquaint myself with the world of international literature. A young man lived in our town who had studied in France and who had a library not only of original French books but also of French translations from the Russian. With the help of a dictionary I began to read Tolstoy, Dostoyevsky, Gogol, Turgenev, and I felt as if I were entering a completely new hemisphere.

Immersing myself in books I forgot for the time being my despondency and my miserable surroundings. At this time the writings of three philosophers also helped me to deepen and sharpen my understanding: Schopenhauer, Nietzsche, Carlyle. Carlyle's theory of "the hero" particularly influenced me and I felt closer to his way of thinking than to that of the two German philosophers. German theorizing had always been alien to me, but I was exalted by the profundities of the Russian literature made known to me for the first time. What I knew of Rumanian literature was that it was pleasant enough, but local and provincial.

In the summer of 1916, Rumania came into the war on the side of Russia, against Germany, and immediately Russian troops started to stream into town on their way toward the frontier. Falticeni was transformed. Gone were the long siestas in the fields and the hours spent reading. The leather factory started to work for the war effort and I no longer had any free time. A brother who had been in the United States for some years suddenly chose just this time to return home. Every able-bodied man in town was called up either for army service or for digging trenches.

In our family, four of the brothers were away and only the youngsters remained at home with our parents. A breath of a different life was brought into the town with each fresh entry of Russian troops: with their exuberance, their wagons and horses, their balalaikas, their singing, and their vodka and food. I can remember one occasion in the winter when a regiment of Cossacks came riding in. Everyone rushed out to greet them. My brother Baruch, who was two years older than I, was asthmatic. He caught cold, as I did too, but his developed into meningitis and four days later he died. Of my brothers, he had been the closest to me in age and sympathy, and his death, the only death in the family I had witnessed, stunned me with grief.

With 1917 the real hardships of war came upon our town: people died in the streets of hunger, a typhus epidemic killed old and young without discrimination. Medical care and medicines were practically nonexistent. The biggest synagogue was turned into a hospital or, more accurately, it served to put a roof over the heads of the sick and dying. Walking to work in the bitterly cold mornings I became accustomed to seeing frozen corpses of those who had died in the night lying out in the streets. It sometimes took weeks before they could be buried, as the ground was so heavily frozen that the old and weak—the only people not in the army—lacked the strength to dig up the hard earth.

One by one, the members of my family fell victims to typhus and, emaciated, dragged themselves around the house. I was the only one who remained in good health. An acquaintance had told me to keep my clothes damp with kerosene as a deterrent to lice, which were the chief typhus carriers. The result was that I smelled vilely of kerosene and developed a skin irritation, but I did not get typhus. The winter of 1917 must have been the worst period our little town ever passed through. It was a luxury to have a candle in the house; as for soap for washing, it did not exist.

In the midst of this deplorable situation an "angel" appeared.

The Most Amazing Character I Ever Met

The name of this "angel" was Munia Posovsky. Suddenly the towns-folk started to smile again and one name was on everyone's lips: Munia Posovsky. Even today, after a full life in which I have met many important and famous people, if I were asked who impressed me most at our first meeting, I would say without hesitation: Munia Posovsky!

I can see him now as clearly as when I first met him: tall, muscular, a rosy-pink face with a big, brown mustache and deep blue, smiling eyes. He was dressed in black, shiny leather—the complete costume, from cap to shoes. Who was he? He was just a soldier in the Russian army but at the same time he was in charge of the provision of meat for the whole Fourth Artillery Corps—60,000 men, who were headquartered at Falticeni.

He was the man who became the savior of Falticeni, the man who managed to bring food and drink to our semi-starving population. If a wedding was to take place, who saw to it that there were sugar and flour, even wine and sweets? Munia Posovsky. If there was going to be a circumcision, who was asked to hold the child but Munia Posovsky, because who else could provide the food and wine for the guests?

Munia could manage everything. He *was* everything. In no time at all he was looked upon as a legendary figure who could work miracles. I remember one day he met me in the street, gave me a bear hug and said, "Happy to meet you, Reuven. I need you. This town is too sad. People are too depressed. We need a theatre to liven things up and you're the person to help me. I shall get hold of the actors and musicians and you'll do the sets."

I thought he must surely be joking. But, no, he was quite serious. Of course, the plan never came to anything, but all the talks we had about it and all the preparations did bring a spirit of fun into the town.

My friendship with Munia meant that at last our house lacked for nothing. We no longer had to worry about trying to obtain bread, meat, kerosene, soap. It seemed as if Munia possessed an inexhaustible store of all that was needed. He used to bring wood in a sleigh and deliver it with a smile, kicking up one leg in a shiny boot in a characteristic gesture. My mother, a rabbi's daughter, tried to find an explanation for the appearance of Munia and his gifts. She said that he must be the Prophet Elijah trans-formed into a Russian soldier in order to help the Jews.

When Munia was in town it seemed as if even Death stayed his hand and sickness decreased. Munia even managed to induce the Rumanian police to undertake the burial of the corpses that used to lie outside the synagogue. He seemed able to influence everybody he met. Even the Rumanian authorities, who usually took no interest in the welfare of the Jewish population, showed him deference and did what he asked them. As for the Jewish community, Munia was their good angel and was loved accordingly.

During this very hard winter of 1917, one of our greatest needs was wood for fuel. The houses were bitterly cold and people went about shivering and blue in the face. Then, one morning, I received a call to a meeting of the Jewish Community Council. What could it mean? I could not understand it——I, the son of Yoel Zeltzer (as everyone called him), one of the poorest men in town, a young man whose only dream was to be an artist, called to sit at the Jewish Community Council table with the "big men" of the town, whom I knew only by name. They were men who would not have considered even passing the time of day with me and now they were asking me to a meeting.

When I arrived I found out that because I was a personal friend of Munia Posovsky, the council members thought I would be able to help the community. They wanted me to persuade Munia to provide wood for us. Falticeni was surrounded by forests and there were always loads of cut timber which waited only for transportation to town, a distance of about fifteen or twenty kilometers.

The council wanted me to take charge of its welfare section and see what I could do. Strangely enough, I did not think their demand impracticable. The first thing of course was to speak to Munia. He responded immediately and went around the neighboring villages with his stick and some bottles of vodka and insisted that those villagers who still had wagons and horses start loading the wood at once and bringing it into town.

I chose the space in front of my father's synagogue as the distribution center and gave him the *mitzvah* of handing out the wood to those who needed it. Every morning the carts or wagons or sleighs arrived from the villages, stacked high with good, dry wood, and there sat my father distributing it equally to everybody. None of the townsfolk knew how the affair had started; nobody knew who would pay for the transportation, but the members of the Community Council strutted about proudly as if all the credit were due to them. Still, the needy knew that their good fortune was due to Munia Posovsky and his friend, Rubin.

Like a fire the news spread through the Russian army in Rumania and to our town: the Russian Government had been overthrown! The first days were full of joy and excitement and hope. Truckloads of children, who had been given cakes and sweets, went careening around singing about the glories of revolution. Naturally, Munia Posovsky was called upon to

SUCCOTH IN JERUSALEM 1926 *oil on canvas* 64 × 50½
collection of the artist

play a part. He was elected head of the Soviet in the Falticeni area. The former commander, a Russian general, was made his assistant, and second in command was the general's former driver. Munia decided the event warranted a general holiday, with a parade in front of the police station. He appeared on the balcony and spoke to the crowd in Russian, Rumanian and Yiddish. But Munia's days of glory were numbered. There were jealousies and quarrels between Russians and Rumanians. The Russians wanted to stop fighting and go back home, while the Rumanians wanted to continue.

One day Munia announced that the Russians were leaving Falticeni. The order was given to the artillery on the Austrian border and suddenly the Russian army with all its armory and equipment turned its face inland to proceed to Odessa. The Rumanians, with their small body of troops encamped in and around Falticeni, decided that the Russian retreat must be prevented at all costs, for otherwise there would be an immediate German invasion. Reinforcements were brought in; trenches were dug around the town to prevent the Russians, our former allies, from coming through. The Jewish community took fright, fearing the worst. The town was full of rumors. The Russian artillery had left the front and was only sixty miles from Falticeni. Sixty thousand Russian soldiers were advancing on the town. The Rumanian troops entrenched in front of Falticeni were determined to show their strength. As soon as the Russians came near enough they opened fire on them. The Russians returned the fire. The noise of cannon and artillery became deafening.

Many of the Jewish population started to pack belongings preparatory to flight. Where they were going to run to they had no idea. I stopped my family from doing likewise; fleeing over the frozen roads meant certain death.

One night the fighting was unusually fierce, the sound of exploding bombs very near. We all wondered why not one bomb had fallen on our part of town, why not one single Jew was wounded. But our Munia-worshipping community soon had the answer. He had given the order that the Jews be spared. So, naturally the bombs flew over the town and not right on it.

After a few days, the fighting turned into a comedy. The Russians decided to accept the Rumanian conditions and surrender! There could not have been more than a few hundred Rumanian soldiers and yet the thousands of Russians surrendered to them! We stood and watched the vanquished Russians marching through the town. They looked very happy to be going home. The ordnance carriages and trucks were covered with all sorts of funny inscriptions. For a bottle of Cognac or vodka one could buy a magnificent horse. By truck, by train, on foot, the Russians left for Odessa.

The war was over! Nobody knew what had happened to Munia or where he was. Then rumors spread that he was in prison, captured by Rumanian troops. A message came from him. How it was delivered

WASHING OF THE HANDS 1936 *oil on canvas* 42 × 35 collection, Mr. and Mrs. Edward G. Robinson, Beverly Hills

nobody knew. But the gist was, "Jews, help me!"

There was a meeting in the synagogue and it was decided to get in touch with the governor of the prison, a local major who was known as a heavy drinker and was said to do anything for money. Word went around the Jewish community: "Give money!" Everybody gave what they could and the money was put into a box and taken to the major. Arrangements were made that the prison guard be occupied elsewhere so that Munia could make his escape, which he did. That was the end of him as far as we were concerned. Nobody in Falticeni saw him again.

But a few years ago in New York, a Jewish actor from Russia with whom I happened to be talking in the Russian Tea Room on 57th Street mentioned the name of Munia Posovsky. From his description, it was indeed the man I had once known. It seemed he was alive and well, living in Odessa, and still interested in the theatre. How much I would have liked to have seen that extraordinary man again and to thank him for all he did for our little town so many years ago, when he appeared like a flame of hope and then disappeared without leaving a trace.

DIKLA 1950 *oil on canvas* $12\frac{1}{2} \times 10\frac{1}{2}$ collection, Mr. and Mrs. N. Bernstein, Dublin

NEAR ABU GOSH 1956 *oil on canvas* 23½ × 29 collection, Ida Kimche Gallery, Tel Aviv

Post-War Days

The war was over and our little town of Falticeni looked like a sick man who has just tottered out of bed. There was no feeling of life nor of any particular season of the year. Everything was grey, monotonous, hopeless. I drifted back to Galatz, my birthplace, but no longer found any sense of contact with the people there. I decided to go to Bucharest, which I had visited as a youngster. That city had felt the full impact of the war. It was a shambles of ruined buildings, destroyed roads and acres of mud, with a depressed and disheartened population. I did find, however, many young students, writers and musicians, people of about my own age who, in spite of their poverty, had the courage of youth, and with them I spent my time. One of my acquaintances let me have the use of an old bathroom in his house where I could work. A room with running water in it meant that I could continue with my experiments in sculpture. I still knew very little of the technique of modeling, but I worked very hard at making busts of people I knew and found that I had a certain aptitude for the work. I especially remember one big figure of a man praying, because it caused me so much difficulty. I was not sure how to set up an armature on which to build up the figure, but after making various experiments with wire and pieces of wood, I managed to construct a workable armature and eventually the piece was cast in plaster. To have it cast in bronze was, of course, out of the question. I did not have the money. The piece was big and bulky and had to be moved from the bathroom to the garden. What happened to it in the end I do not know. All I have today is a photograph.

Working on sculpture and talking to friends in the evenings did not provide a means of livelihood. So when someone suggested I turn my artistic gifts to some commercial purpose, I gave the matter serious thought and started to make designs for furniture and for ornamental objects. When these pieces were exhibited publicly, they created such an impression that every piece was sold.

I then had sufficient funds to be able to rent a livable room. My first purchase afterwards was a pair of shoes, which I needed badly. When spring came I was able to use the garden of the house as a studio. Passers-by would walk in to have a look at what I was doing and sometimes I would ask an interesting-looking individual to pose for me, a request which was never refused.

One day a youngish man, tall, aristocratic-looking, came into the garden. He looked at my pieces of sculpture and also at a batch of canvases which I kept there in case someone was interested in seeing them. He bought two of my paintings, and his understanding of what I was trying to express led to a warm friendship between us. He turned out to be the grandson of one of the major violinists of the state orchestra and bore a well-known name. With the money I received from him I felt as if I had already conquered the town, and I set off at once for Falticeni to share it with my father. I can still remember his peculiar reaction. He found it impossible to believe that anybody could actually earn money from painting. When he was convinced that I had not stolen the money but really had sold paintings, he could not restrain himself from saying, "All right, it is very nice to get so much money for your pictures. But, tell me, where will you find another crazy buyer like that?"

When I got back to Bucharest I started to paint and sculpt with more confidence and hope, and at the same time began to look for other ways of expending my idea and energy. The Jewish writers and musicians in my circle were particularly interested in the theatre, as I was. We came to the conclusion that embarking on a theatrical venture would bring us a lot of pleasure and might also bring in the cash we all needed. There was a good deal of talent in the group and it was not too long before we set up a vaudeville theatre, which every two or three weeks put on a new revue, a combination of music and political satire. We had the stage set up in a garden where people could have a drink and a snack while watching. We became quite well-known and with our resultant success did not find it difficult to obtain financial help from rich acquaintances.

The making of new contacts with known business people brought me an opportunity to deal in leather goods. I saw that it would be possible for me to make some money in this way. I did not relish the thought of giving months of my time to business when I would have been happier painting, but I was so short of funds I felt I could not neglect this opportunity. I was even more successful than I had anticipated, and it was with a considerable amount of money that I again hastened to Falticeni to see and help my family.

My father was delighted that his son was now a businessman, a *mensch* (a real person), as he called me, and not somebody who was trying to live by "scratching a canvas." Having money, brought back to me all my dreams of Paris. The war was over; soon it would be September, when the contestants for the Prix de Rome would begin to "*monter un loge*." How I longed to leave behind me the provincialism of our restricted life and to soar into the azure of freedom!

To my father my returning home with a big sum of money was like a miracle. In a short time his young son had earned more than he in his whole life of toil. This time the money was deposited in a bank. Rumors of my wealth soon began to fly around the town. I had found a gold mine; I had made millions. No sum was too large to be believed.

But in my life, the ups and downs had always repeated themselves with great rapidity. The rumors of my riches did not remain only in Falticeni; they spread far and wide, reaching the town of Harlau where my mother had been born and where her younger brother and sister still lived. They were, of course, poor and always looking for new ways of making money. "Rivile has touched a vein of gold and has millions. So why not try and do something with these millions? Rivile may have made the money but he is no businessman. We are the businessmen who must show him what to do with it."

GALILEAN FISHERMAN 1960 *drawing, pen and ink* collection, Miss Ariella Rubin, Tel Aviv

PRANCING HORSES 1960 *drawing, pen and ink* collection, Motte Gallery, Geneva

I Become a Jam Manufacturer!

And so began a comic chapter of my life: the jam factory. I shall try and relate the story as it is imprinted in my memory.

A young man struggles and dreams and finally manages to collect together sufficient money to allow him to do what he so deeply desires: to go to Paris to paint and to develop himself as an artist. His family will be provided for, so there need be no qualms of conscience. But what happens; that in a short time all his hopes and dreams are destroyed?

I remember it as if it happened yesterday. Toward the end of August, very early in the morning when I was sound asleep in my room, I heard a lot of noise and the sound of heavy boots marching around our balcony. It was perhaps five o'clock but I could not fall asleep again. I saw my father slowly opening the door and peeping in, his face shining with happiness. When he saw I was awake, he sat on my bed and in his warm voice said, "Now, Rivile, if you would like to please me, get up, as some guests have arrived, your mother's brother from Harlau, with some friends, and he has some golden propositions."

Five o'clock in the morning and Uncle Yossele is here with golden propositions. My heart sank. Immediately I had a premonition that my dreams of what I wanted to do were going to fade away. I did not want to upset my father, especially since, for once, he was happy and in a good mood, like a person who feels secure and is able not only to support his whole family but to help others too.

Downstairs I went and greeted Uncle Yossele, a tall, burly man wearing high boots and a fur hat, although it was summer. He explained that he had been traveling all night and that the air was cool. He too was in a lively, gay mood. Drinking a glass of cognac, he said that he was sure he would bring good luck to the house.

Then my father explained the proposition to me: "Uncle Yossele thinks there is a great fortune in jam making—plum jam" (known in Rumania as *powidl*).

I heard for the first time that one can make a fortune from jam. But what had that to do with me? Why wake me up to tell me?

Then Uncle Yossele spoke up. "My dear, you have no experience. You are young. It was very nice that you were able to make some money but now that money has got to be set to work. You can't let money stand idle. Perhaps this is the only time in your life when your father and family have the opportunity to create lasting security for themselves. The idea is simple. Falticeni is the center of the plum-growing district. Plums are dirt cheap, cost practically nothing.

"Just put up a factory and make tons and tons of plum jam for the Christmas trade and then send it all to Galatz, which is the central market. Now that the war is over, people are just dying for jam. The papers say that never before has jam reached such prices. The way I calculate, whatever you will pay here for plums, whatever it will cost to make the jam here, will be only one-tenth of what we can make by selling it.

"Can you imagine what this means? With the money you have, we'll buy plums, put up a factory, start work, then ship the jam off, and in four or five months your father will have security for his old age, I shall have a dowry for my daughters and the whole family will be happy. Only you can save us!"

How can one resist such talk, especially when my father said nothing but looked at me with his hopeful, beseeching eyes. I said to my father, "I don't understand a thing about the matter, but if you think it is right, then put my money into the business. After all, I meant most of it for you. All I want for myself is enough to get me to Paris."

Then the excitement broke out, with hand shaking all around and cries of *mazeltov* (good luck). The jam factory was created. In my ignorance I asked my uncle where the jam factory would actually be located and he said, "It's already here."

He went out to open the gate and let in a one-horse carriage in which were sitting a little man with a pinched sort of face and two half-naked gypsies, shivering in the cool of the morning. There was also a big cauldron which originally had been copper but now looked grimy and black.

My uncle said, "This is the factory and here is my friend Aaronele, a great expert in jam making. This is all we need. A cauldron, a fire and plums. We'll have to get barrels for the jam and you'll have to design a nice emblem and then the gold will start rolling in."

So the "factory" was put into the yard, standing on four blocks of wood, and my brothers and Aaronele and all the neighbors became the plum buyers. After a meeting on strategy it was decided that everybody should set out in different directions so that they should not overbid one another for the plums. "Leave the rest to Aaronele. He's the specialist," said my uncle.

My father took over the finances of the factory and in a day or two plums by the cartload started to come into the yard. There was no time to waste—after all, a gold mine was being uncovered.

It seemed that plums were even cheaper than expected and to celebrate the first purchases, wine and cognac ran like water. A little later, the reports were different. Now plums were rising in price. And the price rose still more, for rumors were spreading that a big jam factory had been opened and needed fruit badly. But the rise in price did not worry Uncle Yossele or the "specialist."

"Whatever price we have to pay, gold will still be coming in."

The aroma of boiling plums permeated the whole of Falticeni. Streams of juice from the cauldron ran down the streets, with half-naked children jumping on the cartloads of fruit and filling up their shirts with plums, with the result that they overate and became ill. The whole town smelled sour, and flies and mosquitoes attacked by the millions. Even the doorknobs of the houses were sticky with plum juice. When people heard that Rubin was making millions out of plum jam, others too started to open small factories. Actually all they did was boil up the fruit, remove the pits and pour the concoction into barrels. Our house was besieged by neighbors looking over the fence to watch the proceedings. The gypsy workers had a fine time playing around with their girls and tossing jam everywhere. It was a regular jam carnival.

The whole affair began to get on my nerves. I left the house and went to stay with a friend, away from the flies and the mosquitoes and the smell of boiling plums. Gloomily I saw my dreams of going back to Paris fading. Nobody bothered to ask my advice any more; they just went on making more and more jam. The money in the bank had been eaten up a long time ago. Not only had the price of plums increased but every official in the town seemed to think he was entitled to some palm-greasing. The bank, however, extended credit to us, for they too believed such a business warranted it.

My father, in his meek way, always asked me to sign bills and not worry. "You'll see, the end will be good."

Then the plums were all used up and the factory stopped work. Hundreds of barrels of jam awaited shipment. There was a meeting of the partners and it was decided that since I had put the money in, it was I who must go to Galatz to sell the jam so as to be sure that the money came straight into my hands before it was divided up. It seemed logical. But what about *my* feelings? I wanted to be off to Paris; I did not give a hoot about the jam. I did not even really care about the money. But my protests were in vain. "It means a delay of only a few months," they told me, "and remember that afterwards your future will be forever secure."

There was no way out but to agree to go to Galatz. I had a new lining of imitation fur put into my old coat so that I would give the impression of a prosperous businessman, and off I went.

The first difficulty was how to ship the stuff. As a result of the war the trains were not yet running properly and freight cars were at a premium. Luckily I was on good terms with the head of the railway station and he promised me a couple of freight cars so that the jam would arrive at the port of Galatz in time for the Christmas trade.

While I was speaking to the railway official, there happened to be an officer there in charge of provisions for the army. Hearing about the dispatch of the jam to Galatz, he offered to buy the lot for the army, naming a price that would have given us a good profit on the investment. I was all for accepting the offer, but I had partners. They would not hear of it and said that we could get double the sum by selling the jam in Galatz. They were supposed to be the businessmen, so I listened to them.

Three days later I was in Galatz. I followed the advice of my partners and went to a certain cafe where the buying agents were in the habit of meeting, and started to sound them out. They tasted the samples and made an offer of ten percent below the officer's proposal.

I wired my partners and the answer came back, "Don't accept. Wait till Christmas when prices will rise."

So I waited, but the barrels of forty tons of jam did not arrive. In the meantime the price of jam dropped. The nonarrival of the goods, I discovered, was due to the fact that the stationmaster of every station on the way to Galatz was waiting for his "rake-off" before he would let the goods through.

When I realized the cause of the delay I took a wad of money and traveled up the line to "oil" the hands of the stationmasters and keep the consignment on the move. Then I went back to Galatz to await the jam's arrival. Business acquaintances advised me to sell as soon as possible, while my partners kept wiring me to hold on. But by then I had enough sense to take no notice of what my partners said, but to sell to all and sundry. I sold for any price offered, for I could see disaster looming ahead. All the fun of the "jam carnival" was over and a rude awakening was coming.

I went back to Falticeni. As long as the weather was cold the jam that was unsold would keep, but soon spring and warm weather would be arriving. And as soon as the weather did turn warm the barrels started exploding in all directions. The police called to say that we had to get rid of the stores and I saw the whole business had come to an end. I closed up the factory and had the remaining jam barrels thrown into the Danube. The money I had brought back from Galatz was just sufficient to cover the overdraft at the bank. My capital had dwindled to nothing. And that was the end of the "gold mine."

My father and the rest of the family did not dare talk to me. All I was intent on were my preparations to leave for Paris, come what may. It did not take long before my uncle Yossele and his Aaronele reappeared in Falticeni. I heard screams and shouts and thumps coming from the living room. My father called me and said that the partners wanted their rights and demanded part of the profits. It was laughable. They knew very well that the whole business had been a disaster, for they had seen the accounts. Yet they wanted their profit! I felt like sinking into the ground or hitting my head against the wall. Why had I ever listened to them?

In such cases, in Jewish families, one did not go to court but put the case up to arbitration. Not wanting my father to see my anger, I listened quietly to the judgment. The three arbitrators came to the conclusion that while there was no denying the lack of profit and the fact that nobody had stolen any money, yet it must be borne in mind that Yossele was the father of three daughters who had to be married off, and he did give his time to the business, while Aaronele, the "expert," had put in months of hard work. They had to be rewarded.

"You, Rivile," the arbitrators said, "are a young man with talent and imagination. You must give these people payment for the work they did and you'll cover this in the same way that you covered the loss, and may God bless you."

The situation struck me as ludicrous. After all the trouble I had and the loss of my money and time, these people had the impudence to ask *me* for a reward. But what could I do? Somehow or other I had to dig the money from the ground, take loans, incur debts and pay my uncle and his "expert." There was no question now of going again to Paris. My mood was black; I was too depressed to paint.

But summer soon came along. The trees blossomed; the grass was lush and green. I started once again to go out in the mornings with my arms full of books and to lie in the meadows reading. My spirits began to revive, my hurts to be healed. I began to forget all about the tragicomedy of the jam factory. Now nobody had the courage to upbraid me for idleness; they all handled me gently. My family and friends realized that I had passed through a very bad time and I was grateful to them for leaving me in peace.

THE SHEPHERD 1932 *drawing, pen and ink*
private collection, Jerusalem

TIBERIAS FISHERMAN FAMILY 1946/54 *oil on canvas* $63\frac{1}{2} \times 51$ collection of the artist

SHEEP-SHEARER 1955 *oil on canvas* 46 × 35 collection, Detroit Museum

My Stay in Czernowitz, 1918–1919

With the annexation of Bukovina to Rumania, Czernowitz, the capital, became the focus of my longings. Although the city was not far from the Rumanian frontier and our little town, it had the atmosphere of a sophisticated, cosmopolitan city. Czernowitz modeled itself on Vienna.

When Rumanian troops left for the city I ventured to travel along with some of the officers I knew. Finding a place to live was a very difficult matter. I did not know anybody there, so, unwillingly, I had to have recourse to the military authorities, where I had good contacts. Armed with a letter from the commandant, I went around the city inspecting such houses as had big windows with a view of the open sky.

At last, in the Theaterplatz, I found the sort of place I was seeking. I walked up four flights of stairs and was received by a family who looked at me with tears in their eyes, regarding me as one of the enemy who were occupying their city.

I tried to be diplomatic and to put as much cordiality as I could into my Yiddish, with the result that I obtained a large room with a wonderful view over the open plaza. As soon as I got settled and was able to prowl around the city, I felt happy and exhilarated as if I had taken a breath of fresh, invigorating air. I was no longer in a little, dingy town of central Europe but in a fine, clean, if bourgeois city, which had a kind of cheerful charm.

People seemed to be gay, always ready for a joke and not inclined to take life too seriously. The good German beer they drank seemed to help keep them warmhearted. As for me, I found it wonderful to have a nice room in a house that had European plumbing, with constant hot water, and even a telephone. It was in high spirits that I set up my easel and started to paint with fervor. The ideas that had been bottled up in me during the years of hardship and war now poured out of me.

I painted a series of canvases that were symbolic in character, with mystical implications, in which the drawing and the composition were the important elements. The colors were mainly pale earth tones: I was still afraid of color.

It was not long after, that I met a painter whose work was arousing interest. His name was Arthur Kolnik, a young man of about the same age as myself, married to a charming young pianist. A quiet man, he lived a simple, orderly life, devoting himself to his work. For the first time I had

a warm friendship with a man of artistic training from whom I could learn the discipline of regular work, and we became inseparable during my stay of about eighteen months in Czernowitz.

I also became acquainted with a number of Jewish Bohemians: writers, poets, actors, who liked the big-town atmosphere of Czernowitz and who had congregated there from Russia, Poland, Bessarabia. At that time I was full of the fire and excitement of my new-found freedom and rejoiced in becoming one of this group, all of whom were bound together by enthusiasm for what was artistically creative, especially by a love of Yiddish literature and the theatre.

A leader of the group was Eleazer Steinberg, already famous as a writer of wonderful Jewish fables. He was a delightful personality with the dynamic power to influence people and the ability to spark one's imagination.

I would spend most of the day working in my studio-room but also found time to enjoy the country around Czernowitz, which was very bucolic, with its little river and shady trees. The *gemuetlichkeit* of the "Viennese" atmosphere was like balm to my harassed mind and spirit. In the evenings "the group" would generally meet in one place or another for endless discussions over a glass of tea or beer. Among the students who gathered around us was Shlomo Bickel, today a well-known Jewish writer and essayist. I found it a stimulating experience to have this free and easy relationship with a number of intellectuals. I, who was born into a family of many children, with many aunts, uncles and cousins, had always felt alone and a stranger until now. But in Czernowitz, among all these strangers, I suddenly felt I was in the midst of a real family.

Our group began to make itself felt in town. Many old Czernowitz residents, cultured people imbued with the standards of Vienna, started to show interest in the Yiddish-speaking group of Jews who brought life into their city. We found that the "old-timers" were happy to be present at our evenings of discussion. It showed that many of these good bourgeois families had a taste for art and lively conversation.

Gradually I started to sell some paintings to them and their friends. It looked as if I were on my way to becoming a real, professional painter. But my restless nature never gave me peace for very long. I was painting, I was writing poetry, I had good friends. But suddenly the desire to be up and doing, changing, moving, started to smolder in me again. Czernowitz seemed too small, too bourgeois. I wanted a wider horizon, a more challenging life.

The visit of an American to my studio brought up, by chance, talk of the great center of New York. For the first time the idea of this fantastic city started to preoccupy my mind. New York, the immense city of skyscrapers, with its large Jewish community, became a burning point of aspiration.

I said nothing to anybody but left for Bucharest to find possibilities about getting to New York. Why I so longed to go there I really did not

GOLDFISH VENDOR 1955 *oil on canvas* 42 × 28
collection, Musée d'art Moderne, Paris

POMEGRANATES NEAR OPEN WINDOW   1965   *oil on canvas*   24 × 32   collection, Mr. and Mrs. Al J. Dreitzer, New York

know. But I had in me the everlasting desire of the wandering Jew to "move on," which gave me no rest.

In Bucharest my old friends encouraged my urge to go to New York and now the topic of conversation became my projected visit to that city. I knew no English, I had no connections there either with galleries or individuals, but yet I felt I must somehow manage to get there.

Back in Czernowitz, my friend Kolnik, seeing how set I was on leaving, asked in his quiet way, "But what shall *I* do?"

Being very attached to him, I immediately said, "You'll come along with me."

Now I was faced not only with finding the money for my own fare but for his too. I did not ask myself what two unknown young painters from Czernowitz were going to do in the "Big City." It reminded me of the incident of years ago when somebody I did not even know asked me to take his grandmother along to Palestine. If I could take an elderly woman, why shouldn't I take my friend Kolnik and make him happy? Then arose the perennial problem: how to get the funds for travelling.

Again I made a trip to Bucharest. It was two years after the war and a certain prosperity had come to the city. I met people who were said to have an interest in art and artists and who might be able to help me. I do not like to remind myself of the horribly unpleasant task of trying to find people to help, or of having to persuade, solicit and "beg," even in a dignified way.

After many unsuccessful attempts, a friend, who still remains like a brother to me throughout some fifty years, Bernard Weinberg, suggested that I talk to his employer, Lazar Margulies, at that time a great figure in finance. Weinberg was himself a great lover of art and music, a talented composer as well as a businessman. He believed I would arouse Mr. Margulies' sympathy, I was doubtful of my success and chary of approaching him, but my dire need gave me strength.

One morning I finally took the courage to go to the big, luxurious offices of Lazar Margulies. Immediately I was impressed by his calm and lordly air. He was so serene, so poised, and yet at the same time he made me feel at ease. He discussed my plight with genuine understanding. Although the request for a loan by a young painter wanting to go to faraway America to exhibit his work and take a colleague along with him, did make Mr. Margulies smile, yet he seemed to like my energetic and straightforward manner.

I asked for a substantial sum, which I calculated would cover Kolnik's and my trip and also give us the means to live till we found our bearings. Mr. Margulies did not keep me on tenterhooks. With a pleasant smile he immediately made out a check for the sum I had requested. I asked him to consider it a loan and I signed a statement obligating myself to return the money to him within a year, free of interest. (For some reason I felt that to repay the loan was a noble gesture, while to pay interest was ugly. Doubtless my attitude could be traced back to the miserable years when my father was always trying to get one loan to repay another and always paying higher and higher rates of interest, keeping him in a state of misery and poverty.) Mr. Margulies took the note and put it in his safe as if to show me he had confidence in my ability to repay the money, though I saw by the twinkle in his eye that he thought this artist a peculiar chap.

I left his office on wings and ran to see Kolnik, who was waiting for me and could not believe his eyes when he saw the check. Now there was nothing to stop our departure. It did not take very long to get the passports and visas and pack the various canvases and pieces of sculpture which, in my naivete I thought would revolutionize the art world. Kolnik and I were now ready to go to New York. When all was ready for departure, Margulies asked me to come and have lunch at his home and meet his family. Such attention from an important, wealthy man to an unknown member of the *Boheme* like myself showed the delicate feelings of this man who did not want me to feel that he was simply handing out charity to me.

At lunch he told me that he had decided to give a farewell dinner at his home—one of the finest mansions in Bucharest—for a few of his friends and such of my personal friends as I would care to invite. I was somewhat disconcerted by his gesture, because although I thought my group consisted of wonderful people, they certainly paid no attention to clothes or manners and had probably never sat at such an elegant table. How would they appear to the rich financiers whom Mr. Margulies was inviting? Nevertheless I did invite my friends, begging them to remember to comb their hair and clean their shoes.

On the appointed evening I went out to a suburb to fetch two of my best friends, Moti and his wife, who had often treated me to a meal when I was short of cash. It was a horrible night, blustery, with rain and sleet. Because of the weather the tramways had stopped running and there did not seem to be any way of getting to the dinner. I stood outside my friends' house, hoping to find some means of transport. Then, as in a fairy tale, appeared a fine landau drawn by two beautiful horses. I saw that it was empty and made a sign to the coachman to stop. I took a big bill out of my pocket and told him that it was his if he would drive me to my destination. It so happened that he was going in our direction anyway, since the carriage was one of the royal vehicles which was returning to the palace, and Mr. Margulies' house was not far from there.

I called Moti and his wife and we all sat comfortably inside the luxurious carriage, which was upholstered in silk and had curtains over the windows. Moti, who had a great sense of humor, just sat there quietly as to the manner born and said to me, "Can you believe it? In this terrible weather there still are people who must walk!" This from him who never rode anywhere but always walked to save money!

At any rate, the dinner was a great success and my friends of the *Boheme* all behaved with the utmost decorum.

En Route to the U.S.A.

We were planning to take a cargo ship which made fortnightly trips from Galatz to Naples. I had a talk with the captain to try and persuade him to allow two artists going abroad for an exhibition to travel more cheaply. He did more than I asked: he allowed us to travel free, including our numerous cases and packages!

When we arrived at Naples I felt in a generous mood and took a room at a good hotel with a wonderful view of the bay. Kolnik and I walked about the town, enjoying its colorful life. I booked passage for us to New York, third class, of course, on an Italian liner named, oddly enough, the *Dante Alighieri*. This was the second time in my life that the name of the great poet had figured in my travels.

The Rumanian boat we had come on was still in port and I had left my cases of paintings and sculpture on board, assuming that when the time came to board our next ship, the only procedure required would be to have cases moved over. The day before the Italian liner was due to sail, our cases were put on board and the purser, with whom I had already made friends, said he would find a good place to store them. It was already understood that there would be no extra charge.

Our last day in Naples, Kolnik and I were like children, going from museum to piazza and from cafe to cafe. It seemed to me that Naples had never looked so fascinating. Little did I know of the trouble in store for us.

Standing in line to board our ship, we had to pass the U.S. immigration officer, since after the war there was an enormous influx of immigrants to America. And although the visas of Kolnik and myself stated that we were going as visitors, the officer did not take this seriously. The Americans assumed that every European, especially any Jew and more especially any Rumanian Jew, must be using the term "visitor" as camouflage for "immigrant."

To my great disappointment, the officer said that we could not board this ship, because a new law had been passed which stated that all passengers from eastern Europe had to go via Le Havre in France, and there pass twenty days in quarantine.

There was the *Dante Alighieri* looming over us, large and stately in the noon sunshine, and due to sail in a few hours, and here were we, informed that we could not leave on the ship, which already had my paintings on board! But there was nothing to be done. The shipping agent at once offered to refund the money for our tickets. But the immigration officer pointed out that that would not be sufficient. The agent had sold us the tickets without acquainting himself with the law and he would therefore have to refund not only the money but pay for our trip to Le Havre and for our stay in Naples as well. Afraid perhaps of legal unpleasantness, the agent paid all the charges the American officer had requested, so at least I did not lose anything financially.

I then ran up the gangplank to explain the situation to the ship's purser and to give him instructions as to what to do with my cases on arrival in New York. But new complications awaited me. The purser was there with my cases, but so were some policemen too. The sailor who had moved the cases from the Rumanian to the Italian ship was down on his knees, weeping and pleading for mercy. It seems the Italian port authorities had discovered that cases containing merchandise had been put aboard the transatlantic liner without passing through customs. This meant they were considered to be contraband goods. Not only that, but, since the war, such goods were known by an even more ominous name: "*contrabande de guerra.*" The police were there with a warrant for my arrest and that of the boatman. It was a frightening moment and I was extremely upset to hear the boatman crying out that he was the father of eight children and that it was I who had put him into this terrible quandary.

I asked who had made the indictment. One of the police officers said, "The head of customs." I asked where the customs office was and he pointed to a large building on the wharf. Without another word, I raced down the gangplank toward the designated building. The policemen dashed after me. I ran into the building, and, assuming that the director must have his office upstairs, ran up to the third floor, with the policemen, sweating and swearing, behind me. I ran from door to door and at last saw the sign: "Office of the Director."

I stormed into the room without knocking and saw a gentleman being helped on with his coat by another man. The gentleman turned round, astonished at the intrusion. And who should it be but Piombino, an old friend from Genoa, who had been head of the general customs house when I was working for the leather factory. He greeted me warmly, as if he thought I had come to see him on a friendly visit. Without more ado, I explained that I was looking for the director of customs. "But I am the director," he said.

"Well, you sent a warrant for my arrest."

"What warrant and what arrest?" he asked.

I explained what had happened and that my cases contained only paintings that I was taking over for an exhibition and that I did not know that they had to pass customs. He threw off his coat, took the warrant and wrote and signed a statement which he then stamped, asking me for five lira. He gave orders that I should be taken back to the ship and my cases opened. If they did contain paintings, then the matter was in order. So back to the ship we went, the policemen now treating me with more

SAFED FAMILY 1923 *oil on canvas* 32 × 26 collection, Tel Aviv Museum, Lowenthal Bequest, Gift of Mrs. Esther Rubin, Tel Aviv

respect. The purser opened the cases and the first thing he saw was my self-portrait looking up at him. So the cases were nailed down again and sent to the hold, the boatman was released and the policemen departed. The purser smiled at the happy ending. I then told him that I was not going to travel on this ship and I gave him a note addressed to the man who had been my first purchaser of paintings in Bucharest, and was now director of the Rumanian Bank in New York, the only person I knew there. It was to him the cases should be delivered. I liberally compensated the purser for his cooperation and then returned to shore while the ship set sail for America.

I did not return to Naples very happily, for I was disturbed by the thought that my paintings were floating to New York without me, to be consigned to someone who was not even expecting them.

But little by little, I began to realize that what had happened was not such a calamity. I still had a few weeks free before I was to take the ship from Le Havre so I decided to give myself the treat of a visit first to Paris. Great was my disappointment when I learned from the shipping company's office in Paris that I had to go immediately to the U.S. immigration authorities in Le Havre and stay there under supervision for the whole of the quarantine period. Luck, though, was with me, and the American doctor in charge of quarantine was a most amiable man who made no difficulties about giving me permission to return to Paris, with the under-standing that I appear in Le Havre for my final examination at least one day before the ship sailed. In Paris, I spent most of my time seeing paintings, and I also bought myself a little book, *Do You Speak English*, which I learned almost by heart preparatory to my arrival in the United States.

The journey across the Atlantic was uneventful, but I lived in a state of perpetual excitement, anticipating the great events that I felt were awaiting me in the New World. I did many caricatures and sketches of the passengers and crew, and scenes of ship life. A few days before the ship was due to dock, the captain asked if I would like to have an exhibition on board to aid the Sailors' Welfare Fund. I agreed, and I believe that a good sum of money was realized for the Fund.

I learned from one of the ship's officers that my arrival in New York would be facilitated if I had some relative there who could meet me. I remembered that my father had a brother somewhere in the United States. On a "hunch," I asked for the New York telephone directory and started looking for the name "Zelicovici." With the officer's assistance I wired him of my arrival, asking him to meet me at the landing pier and adding that both of us should wear a white flower in our lapels.

FLOWERS ON MY WINDOW 1950 *oil on canvas* 36 × 29 collection, Sir Edward and Lady Beddington Behrens, London

Arrival in New York

The arrival of immigrants from eastern Europe has been described so often by pens more gifted than mine that I will spare the reader a detailed account. The sight of the Statue of Liberty moved me almost to tears as it has done countless others. The sight of the fantastic canyons of buildings with their thousands of windows looking down on me was overpowering. I felt they were leaning on me, pressing me deeper and deeper into the ground till I was reduced to nothing.

Suddenly I felt completely lost. Why had I come to New York? Whatever would I do in this immense city? Who cared about another unknown coming to these shores? I tried to give myself some courage. I joined the long line of people in front of the immigration officer. An hour of agony. So many questions, while the official looks at one as if nothing one says is the truth.

When my turn came I was asked if I spoke English. "Yes," I replied in a deep voice, only praying that I would not be asked questions I could not answer.

"Have you any money?"

"Yes."

"What do you intend to do here?"

"I am a painter and am going to have an exhibition of my work."

"Fine, move along . . . "

I nearly fainted with relief. Then came Kolnik's turn. The same question.

"Do you speak English?" Very honestly my poor friend said, "No."

True, he knew less than I did, but he could at least have replied, "Yes," I thought anxiously. When asked if he had any money, he again answered, "No," knowing that I held the money.

The result was that Kolnik was sent off to Ellis Island and I went down to the pier a free man. I was informed I could visit him the next day with a lawyer and that he would almost certainly be released.

Waiting among the people who had come to meet relatives or friends was a tall man resembling my father and wearing a white flower. I went up to him and he proved to be my uncle. After a cordial greeting he took me to his home for a meal and a night's rest.

When I saw the lower East Side where he lived I could hardly believe my eyes. It was hot, the beginning of summer, and the streets and houses

SILENT PRAYER 1942 *oil on canvas* 46 × 35½ collection, Mr. and Mrs. Arthur Rubinstein, Paris

OLD OLIVE TREES 1967 *oil on canvas* 24 × 29 collection, Mr. and Mrs. Arthur Lipper III, Geneva

began learning our way about the vast city and trying to understand the language.

My first visit, of course, was to the bank director to whom my paintings had been consigned. I was rather worried about how he would receive me, but he was most cordial and told me that my cases were in the bank vault and could remain there until I had a place to put them. This was the first bit of good news and I felt encouraged.

Kolnik and I continued to explore the city on foot and became valiant walkers. One day we went from the Battery up the whole of Broadway, and, after walking all day and all night, occasionally resting on a bench, found ourselves in the Bronx! We used to study the posters and advertisements to try to improve our English, as well as to find out what was happening in this city where everything was so new and strange to us. The huge newspapers impressed us enormously, especially the Sunday editions which seemed to weigh a ton and conveyed an idea of the greatness and richness of the country. But I could not understand very much of what I read. It was the comics that appealed to me most; "Mutt and Jeff" and "Krazy Kat" soon became my "friends."

From an advertisement I learned that on a certain evening there was to be a big Jewish entertainment in an armory and I suggested to Kolnik that we go there. I found the program of the evening intriguing: 200 cantors would be singing "Eli Eli"—a Hebrew song, really a lament, that was then very popular in Jewish circles—and boxing champion Benny Leonard would give a display of a few rounds. He, of course, was the great attraction of the evening and thousands of people must have come to the huge building.

I walked about, trying to appear as American as I could, eating hot dogs and ice cream like everybody else. But people kept glancing at me, the intruder, the foreigner, and I suppose I did look exotic and peculiar. Then a woman came to me and, speaking Yiddish, introduced herself as Bertha Kling, a poetess. I gave her my name and said that I was a painter. It seemed that a Yiddish newspaper either from Rumania or Paris had published an item about my going to New York, so that my name was not completely unfamiliar to her.

We began a friendly conversation and she then introduced me to some of her friends: writers, musicians, journalists, who were apparently in New York Jewish circles. After the program we went to the Cafe Royal, the headquarters of the Yiddish intelligentsia. From that time on I was accepted among this group and while I was still as far off as ever from an exhibition, I felt much more at home. The companionship of these people who spoke "my language" reminded me of the group I had left behind in Czernowitz. Bertha Kling's house soon became a sort of haven, and its friendly atmosphere gave me a feeling of well-being, while her husband, a physician, welcomed me with equal kindness.

My friend the bank director, whom I saw occasionally, invited me to spend a few days in his luxurious house on Fifth Avenue, opposite the

Overleaf: JERUSALEM, THE GOLDEN 1946/66 *oil on canvas* 38 × 64 collection, Mr. and Mrs. Philip Vogelman, New York

were crowded with people, most of them in a state of undress and all talking at once. The noise was deafening. Though my uncle was not poor, he was far from rich and he managed to get along.

He had a three-room apartment on the fourth floor of a tenement building, which I later learned was known as a "railway apartment." In the front it had two windows onto the street and one window in the kitchen, which was in the back; the middle rooms were dark and enclosed. Toilet facilities were on the landing and were shared by two other families.

I was stunned! Falticeni was only a small, poor town, but at least the rooms had windows which let in the fresh air, and while the washing and toilet facilities were out in the yard, there at least were no neighbors standing in line for the door to open.

So this was New York? And it was for this that I had longed? How would I ever be able to arrange an exhibition and find myself? I thought with fury of the man who had first given me the idea of going to the United States. Then I began to remember that from aboard ship I did see some big, shining skyscrapers. There must be another America too and it is that America, the great America, that has earned the respect of the Old World, that I must discover.

I thanked my uncle for his kindness but said that I would prefer to take a room in a hotel, since my friend would soon be released from Ellis Island and we were going to stay together. Perhaps my uncle found me ungrateful for refusing his hospitality, but nevertheless he took me over to a hotel called "The Sagamore," not far from where he lived. It did not look very inviting, but I suppose my uncle thought it was good enough for an artist. An artist is not worth much; he is not a banker or a businessman or a bookkeeper. He is just a lazy "layabout" who smears paint on canvas. All this I could read plainly in my uncle's eyes although he said nothing.

My room was on the third floor, at the end of a long corridor. There was no elevator. Opposite the window I could see the hotel sign in red and green, changing color every second. The maid who showed me the room said, "It's a wonderful room. You won't need to put on the electricity as you have the outside lights day and night." Wonderful, I thought, to have to live in a room with "Sagamore" flickering into my eyes every moment. But I made no complaint. Such, I thought, is the U.S.A. and I have to put up with it.

The cooking smells of hamburgers and steak floated up to my room and made me lose my appetite. So I went out and obtained a plan of the city and started to learn what was "uptown" and "downtown," "east side" and "west side," and how to travel on the subway without getting lost. It all seemed very complicated.

As soon as possible I went to Ellis Island with a representative of the Jewish Immigrants' Association and my uncle, who was an American citizen. The necessary statements were made and attested to, and twenty-four hours later Kolnik was released. I was happy to have him with me and life in the "Sagamore" became pleasanter with a partner. We soon

Metropolitan Museum. A magnificent mansion, it had once been owned by a Greek princess. Staying with him gave me yet another insight into American life. The adjustment to so many new aspects of life was bewildering and I began to feel that everything was too much for me. With the advance of summer the heat grew greater and New York became a real inferno. The noise, the great numbers of people, the rushing, and the long distances that I was always covering on foot, began to overcome my normal resilience. It seemed to me that everything around me was in a state of turmoil, with the sweating masses of humanity trying to catch their breath in the tainted air. I had already been in New York for two months and had not put a brush to canvas for I had no place to work.

Again I started to feel that I was wasting my time. I felt I had to find a place outside New York where I could paint until the time came when I was ready to contact art galleries and dealers. The summertime was a dead period in the art world of New York.

One evening at Mrs. Kling's I started to talk about the possibility of creating a "kibbutz" (the communal agricultural settlements were just then taking root in Palestine). Some of those present liked the idea and suggested I try and find a suitable place in the country. I certainly knew nothing of the suburbs or country around New York but I thought the name "Far Rockaway" sounded attractive so I concentrated on that area.

I eventually came upon an old house that had been unoccupied for some years and the real estate agent told me that we could have it for very little money. The repairs needed and the repainting we could do ourselves. Kolnik and myself, plus five couples, made up the group. We each contributed some money and in a very short time we had patched and cleaned up the house and managed to borrow enough furniture to make it habitable. It was situated about 200 yards from the sea, which I enjoyed so much.

For a time I felt contented. I had time for painting and could go bathing and enjoy the fresh air and sunshine. Kolnik and the others were equally delighted, feeling it was wonderful to have a place to themselves and be free to do what they liked. So, a few months passed in work and play. We had frequent visitors, among whom were the writer Sholem Asch and his wife, who were particularly taken with the creative atmosphere of the "kibbutz." Other writers known in Jewish circles, such as Levick, Reisen, Schwartz and Auerbach also came to see us.

But the predominantly literary atmosphere in which I lived was not the right influence for my artistic development. I started to feel that I was too much under the yoke of the spoken and written word. Previously my dreams had been full of color and movement and pictorial designs; now they were filled with stories and verbal rhythms. My feeling of being "lost" returned and as summer neared its end I began to feel that I was heading for a nervous breakdown. I could see no end to the road I was taking.

SPRINGTIME IN GALILEE   1963/64   *oil on canvas*   29 × 36   private collection, Mexico City

The other members of the "kibbutz" began to return to the city and Kolnik and myself were left alone. The shabby, ghostly house in Far Rockaway began to give us both the chills. We closed it up and returned to New York. I visited my bank director friend and he cordially invited me to stay with him again.

It was the beginning of autumn and the art world was reviving. An exhibition of works by Van Gogh and Gauguin opened at the Metropolitan Museum, the first New York showing of these great artists. Seeing their paintings injected new life into my veins. A storm of disapproval burst out from the public, who found the works difficult to understand. While the animosity of the public distressed me, at the same time I found it thrilling that the vital creativity of these artists, both of whom were dead, could still generate so much feeling; it was a sign of their power. The whole experience made me feel that I would find my way out of the dead end at which I had arrived.

Toward the end of September my friend invited me to lunch with a guest of his from Paris, named Dewald. This visitor was a collector with a fine understanding of art. He invited me to spend a weekend at his country home on the Hudson, where I literally feasted on Impressionist paintings and drawings. He became interested in my work and told me that he had a friend who was the finest art connoisseur and critic then in the United States. His name was Alfred Stieglitz. He said that he would try and get Stieglitz to see my work, as he thought Stieglitz might be able to bring me before the public.

A little later I received a telegram from Lake George, where Stieglitz was vacationing, saying that he could come and see my paintings. What excitement, what joy! I received him in the vaults of the bank where my paintings were stored.

"An unusual place to show paintings," he remarked. Stieglitz was a small man with a gentle expression and greyish mustache, very quietly dressed, in contrast to the usual American fashion, and I noticed that his hat had a hole in the crown through which his grey hair showed.

He looked attentively at my canvases and questioned me about my life and ideas. It made me proud to see that he was giving serious consideration to my work and I awaited his verdict with eagerness. I could hardly believe that it was I, an unknown young man from a small town in Rumania, who was showing his paintings to the famous Stieglitz, who was the first to introduce modern art to America in the celebrated Armory Show of 1913.

As we were speaking, he reached for the telephone and dialed a number. My heart leaped when I heard the name, "Duveen." Speaking simply but with authority, Stieglitz said that he would very much like Duveen to come over to the address he gave him as there were some paintings he would like him to see. The situation seemed to become more and more unreal. Now it was Duveen, the emperor of art dealers, who was coming to inspect my work!

Not more than half an hour passed when Duveen, most elegantly dressed, with white spats, arrived and greeted Stieglitz in a friendly manner. Stieglitz showed him certain paintings and suggested he buy two of them. I no longer remember what canvases he chose, but I do recall that he gave Stieglitz a check and told his chauffeur to take the paintings to his car. Then Duveen sat down at the telephone and called up Mitchell Kennerley, the then director of the well known Anderson Gallery in New York. He told him about his meeting with Stieglitz and said that he wanted him to exhibit the work of two young painters, Rubin and Kolnik, at the Anderson Gallery.

The whole episode put me into a state of near delirium. It had all happened so quickly and so unexpectedly.

A couple of days later the gallery's secretary came with photographers and some press people. The whole affair was no dream but a fact. I could not find words with which to thank Stieglitz for the opportunity he had given me and arrangements were made for us to meet again.

KING DAVID PLAYING THE HARP 1960 *drawing, pen and ink*
collection Binet Gallery, Jerusalem

First Exhibition in New York, 1920

The whole thing seemed miraculous to me. Suddenly I had stepped into the ranks of professional painters with an exhibition at the well-known Anderson Gallery, sponsored by Alfred Stieglitz! The wheels of promotion and publicity were set turning: articles and photographs in the papers, interviews and announcements of the coming show. A new world opened in front of my eyes. I was in a state of continuous excitement. The stir which the coming exhibition created among my friends and acquaintances added to the tense atmosphere.

The Rumanian Ambassador to Washington was then Prince Bibesco, who was married to a daughter of former British Prime Minister, Herbert Asquith. He sent a letter of congratulation to me and offered to give his patronage to the exhibition, in view of my Rumanian citizenship. Actually my paintings had little to do with Rumania or its art traditions; they were influenced mostly by my sojourn in Palestine and my feelings about Judaism and its mystical aspects. But the Prince invited me to lunch with him in New York and, on the advice of Stieglitz, I gratefully accepted his patronage of the exhibition, which was set for November, 1921.

Prince Bibesco told me that by coincidence his mother-in-law, the famous Margot Asquith, was visiting America and would be on hand at the opening of the exhibition. She was a much-courted and witty personality and her appearance would certainly add great social luster to the occasion.

I saw Stieglitz nearly every day in the gallery; he had a section there called "The American Place," where he showed the works of his artists: John Marin, Georgia O'Keefe, Hartley and Dove. Being able to spend time with Stieglitz was a real experience for me. For the first time I listened to informed criticism and to wise understanding of art and artistic life. In a few weeks I learned more from him than in all the ten years since I had left home and gone to Jerusalem, Paris, and Italy.

Due to the presence of Lady Asquith, the opening was a great social affair. Everybody there seemed to know one another and chatted and laughed over their cocktails, while I stayed in a corner with Stieglitz. Nobody bothered to say anything to me and it was rather as if a party for Lady Asquith were taking place and not an exhibition of paintings. Happily for me, Stieglitz kept me from depression by his lively remarks and the sensible way he looked at the whole matter. Once the cocktails were finished, the crowd disappeared. Stieglitz patted me on the back and philosophically said, "So that's that."

The society magazine, *Town and Country*, gave a lot of space to the exhibition, with stories and reproductions, and so did many newspapers. But I had hoped that the opening would be an artistic and not a social occasion, and I felt very sad and disillusioned. It seemed to me that the visitors had hardly looked at the paintings, and, as for buying any, obviously that was the last thing that entered their heads.

The twenty days of the exhibition brought many viewers but what impression, if any, it made in art circles I did not know, as I had no contact with them. Stieglitz himself was encouraging and gave me a book by Marsden Hartley called *Adventures in Art*. In the inscription—written in German, as my English was still not too good—he underlined one phrase, "I wish you only *Ausdauer* (persistence), the rest you have." At the time I doubt whether I really grasped what he meant, but since then his words have rung in my ears and heart like the sound of my father's prayers in the synagogue.

Members of the Jewish community, although few of them were true art lovers, did purchase some of my paintings and I suppose I should have been proud and happy at what little success I had. Instead, I had a feeling of disappointment, of blighted hopes. It was not that I had expected big sales, but I suppose in my heart I had longed for more artistic appreciation, and I found little understanding among those who came to the exhibition. The effect upon me was to make me lose confidence in my future even though the newspaper critics had been kind to me. When I look back on that period, the beginning of the "twenties," I see what a tremendous development has since taken place in the understanding and appreciation of art in the United States. It was nearly fifty years ago and a strong feeling for the value of artistic creation had not yet been awakened.

Return to Rumania

After covering all our expenses, Kolnik and I still had enough funds for our return home. I sent some money to my family and also paid off the debt to my "Maecenas" in Bucharest who had given me the loan exactly a year ago to the day. The intricate monetary situation after the war made this payment very easy, for whereas when I took the loan it was worth about $ 3,000, I was able to repay it with about $ 200. My banker friend arranged the repayment and seemed to think I would be more sensible to turn to money speculation deals than to go on painting. Perhaps from one point of view he was right. But he didn't realize that painting was an inner compulsion of mine which could not be gainsaid.

Kolnik and I were a happy pair the day we bought our return tickets to Rumania. I left a number of paintings and some sculpture with different friends in New York, which I thought they would either try to sell or keep for me. I was in such a hurry to go that I did not even make a list of their names and addresses, and to this day I do not know what became of these works. There was one big painting which I particularly liked, called "Resurrection," of which I at least have a photograph.

My uncle, who in the meantime had become proud of this "greenhorn," as he called me—who had managed to become known and mix with "important people" on Park Avenue—thought it unbelievable that I wanted to return to Rumania. The only person who understood my decision was Alfred Stieglitz. He was my "guru" and his remarks were like Holy Writ to me. Thus ended my first adventure in the New World in 1921. I left not disillusioned but rather bewildered and dissatisfied. Yet I think that even then in the depths of my heart I realized that I would one day return and come to value and better understand the country and its people, and on my many later visits I did come to comprehend and love the vitality and the "urge to know" which are so characteristic of young America. But my friend Kolnik was completely disillusioned and he never attempted to go back.

On the way home we stopped off in Paris for a brief stay. How could anybody by-pass Paris? But having taken Kolnik away from his wife and home in Czernowitz, I felt I had to safely return him there. He, however, suggested we first stop off in Vienna, where his parents were living. After the rush and bustle of New York life, Vienna seemed beautiful but sleepy, while the misery and poverty brought about by the war and the devaluation of money gave a sinister atmosphere to the city and everybody told us that it was nothing like pre-war Vienna.

When we finally arrived in Czernowitz, Kolnik and I were greeted like returning victors by our old friends. In my heart, however, I asked myself whether it had all been worthwhile. What I have said about my year in America may sound as if luck had been with me and that the end was crowned with success. But in reality, the loneliness of my soul and the bitter days and nights when I felt forlorn and utterly lost in the immensity of the city, made my time there for the most part despairing and unhappy.

Going home to Falticeni to see my parents, I found the situation unchanged and I did not stay long but went again to Bucharest. Now I had sufficient means to get a suitable studio. I found an empty garage which could be turned into an adequate studio and I at once started to work with enthusiasm. There was a change in my painting; it became clear and colorful. Soon old friends and new acquaintances among artists and writers started to visit me and the "garage-studio" with its big stove in the middle became a meeting place where many discussions were held and many poems recited.

At the end of a year I had amassed enough canvases for an exhibition, and I showed my paintings in my garage-studio. The reviewers acclaimed what they called "a revolutionary manifestation in art." I was pleased with the success but my pent-up energies as usual began to urge me to make another move. I was still hungering for Palestine and soon an occasion to go there arose with the departure of a ship taking hundreds of pioneers, mostly Russian refugees, from Galatz to Jaffa. Since I had already lived in Palestine, it was suggested that I be the leader of the group. Elated, I felt that I was about to return to my true home.

The young people were a lively group, filled with zeal to lead a pioneering life in the Promised Land. Their enthusiasm and idealistic spirit were inspiring. My special task was to prepare the documents for the debarkation. To enable the young people to land without trouble, I had to arrange a number of "marriages." If a girl had a passport with an immigration permit and a young man had none, or vice versa, then a marriage was arranged between them so that they could both enter Palestine legally. The ship's captain was always willing to perform a marriage ceremony at any time and every ceremony was the occasion for drinks and jollity. When we arrived at Jaffa we had a whole boatload of newlyweds. The representative of the Zionist Agency who came to meet us was the late Joshua Gordon, who afterward became a good friend of mine. I was able to hand over the "cargo" in excellent condition and then I went off straight to Jerusalem.

Again to the Promised Land

In the interim of ten years since I had last been in the city a tremendous change had taken place. In 1912, Palestine had been a backward Turkish province with Turkish gendarmery and soldiers in the streets, who on Fridays paraded around the Jerusalem Citadel to the sound of Turkish marches. But when I came back in 1922, it was as if to a new country. The Balfour Declaration had opened the doors to Jewish immigration and a Jewish Agency was working in Jerusalem. Great Britain was the mandatory power and English was heard everywhere.

While in New York, I had come in contact with a number of personalities in the Zionist movement, including Dr. Shmarya Levin, Nahum Sokolow, Jabotinsky, and two young able and enthusiastic workers for the Zionist cause, Gershon Agronsky and Meyer Weisgal. The former was to become the editor of the *Palestine Post* (now *Jerusalem Post*) and, later, Mayor of Jerusalem, while Meyer Weisgal, after spearheading the creation of the Weizmann Institute of Science, became its president and leading spirit. My meeting with these men took place at the New York offices of the Zionist organization, when I went armed with a letter from Nahum Sokolow to Dr. Levin, asking the latter to do what he could to help me. I always hated "traipsing" from place to place with letters of introduction beseeching help, but there were times when such action was unavoidable. Nobody seemed to have any time to tell me where I could find Dr. Shmarya Levin, so I sat patiently waiting in the anteroom. Then someone came over and asked me in Yiddish what I wanted. His name was Khouna. He was one of the first Zionist workers and a well-known character. I handed him my letter and to my astonishment he tore it up, saying "Why are you going to ask Shmarya Levin for help? He doesn't know anything about painting."

At that moment Gershon Agronsky passed, and hearing some of the discussion, he took me into his office where at last I heard a word of sympathy. But what made the meeting especially notable for me was that on the wall I saw the first poster printed by the Zionist organization after the Balfour Declaration, appealing for funds for Palestine. It was a poster which I had designed!

A couple of years earlier, a visitor to my studio in Czernowitz had talked about the setting up a fund-raising institution for Palestine, and since I had lived there he had suggested I design a poster. We found the slogan "Give Us the Key," and I drew a sketch of Palestine locked behind a big iron gate. At the bottom were the words, "Give Us the Key—Open the Gate." I handed over my finished design to my caller and he promised I would receive a fee. But I saw neither him nor any money, nor did I know what had happened to my poster until I saw it on the wall of Agronsky's office.

When Agronsky realized I was the poster artist, he was delighted, and it was through him that I met Dr. Levin and Meyer Weisgal. From that time on I attended meetings and other events of the Zionist organization, and when I opened my exhibition at the Anderson Gallery, the heads of the movement came in force to honor me.

When I returned to Jerusalem I therefore had direct access to the heads of the Zionist Mission, as it was then called, and among the personalities with whom I was able to become acquainted were Israel Sieff, now Lord Sieff of Brimpton; the late Brigadier Kisch, then Colonel; the then Dutch Consul, Van Vriesland; the noted lawyer and author, Harry Sacher.

I also quickly got to know artists and intellectuals there through my friendship with the sculptor Aaron Melnikoff, who had been in Jerusalem since 1918 and had been a volunteer in the Jewish Brigade. I soon felt at home and began to master Hebrew, and life became full of activity and interest. I managed to get a nice, large room in the house of a Bokharan family living in the Yemin Moshe quarter. Melnikoff, who lived in romantic fashion on the walls of Jerusalem over the Damascus Gate of the Old City, allowed me to use his studio when I needed it. His home, with its large, comfortable rooms, was a focal point for the young Jerusalemites. Daily there were discussions with other artists who too were trying to find a place for themselves in art. But we were not serious all the time: there were gay evenings of singing and drinking and donkey rides by moonlight over the surrounding hillsides. We were all young, and life was full of hope and expectation.

Among the officials of the Mandatory Government I knew Sir Ronald Storrs, Governor of Jerusalem, who was interested in music and art, and Edwin Samuel, who was the son of the High Commissioner Sir Herbert Samuel and had recently married Hadassah, daughter of the Grasovskys, friends of mine from Tel Aviv.

After some time, I went to Tel Aviv to see what had happened with that town which had been little more than a few houses and a couple of streets when I knew it in 1912. There I found a lively, bubbling atmosphere and tremendous building activity. My younger brother, who had come to Palestine a couple of years earlier, was working there as a builder. I felt

OLD OLIVE FOREST 1967 *oil on canvas* 38 × 64 collection of the artist

that I too should stay in Tel Aviv, for I fell in love with the youthful character of the city, and the sea had always held an attraction for me.

Moving there, my first home was a tent on the sand dunes. I brought in my painting gear, put a carpet and a trestle bed down on the floor, hung my clothes on a line stretched across part of the tent, and started to look around for sitters. The milkman, the porters, the carriers of *ziv-ziv* (sand for the building trade) were my models, as were, in fact, anybody I could induce to sit for me. I loved the look of the Yemenites sitting near my tent and of their goats who pushed their heads under the canvas from time to time. Among the painters whom I met at that time were Israel Paldi who had come from Russia as a teen-ager, Leo Lubin from the United States, and Jaffa-born Ziona Tagger. Then there was the dancer Agadati, and the Grasovsky and Isaac Katz families—every one of us enjoying the present and full of plans for the future.

After some months I found an old house which had once been a school, near Jaffa. I was able to rent it for next to nothing, and with the help of my brother and some other young people, cleaned and painted it and put it into some order. It became a sort of "Kibbutz Rubin," occupied by half a dozen other young men, with a Yemenite girl as our housekeeper. During the day, the others went off to work, and then I had the house to myself and could paint without interruption.

Rumania was forgotten, New York far away. The literary and poetic influences disappeared from my work. In Palestine there was sunshine, the sea, the *halutzim* (pioneers) with their bronzed faces and open shirts, the Yemenite girls, and children with enormous eyes. A new country, a new life was springing up around me. I felt the sap of creative energy rising in me too. I threw away all the ideas I had derived from the Bezalel Art School and the Paris Beaux Arts. The world around became clear and pure to me. Life was stark, bare, primitive. I did not feel burdened by problems and I found it easy to work. I painted as a bird sings, without effort, joyfully. In these years of 1923 and 1924 I began really to live in my work. It was a true expression of myself.

First Exhibitions in Jerusalem and Tel Aviv

By the beginning of 1924 I had a large group of canvases which I wanted to exhibit. A talk I had with Sir Ronald Storrs gave me the idea of exhibiting at the old Citadel of David in Jerusalem. I used to go to Jerusalem occasionally and stay in my old room in Yemin Moshe. I remember painting a family group there and also a study of a young girl, Ada, a beautiful little creature of about seven. The painting turned out well and later in Paris was sold to the writer Konrad Bercovici of New York.

Sir Ronald suggested I obtain the key to the Citadel and see whether it would be possible to hold an exhibition there. It was a massive piece of architecture and the place had probably not been used for over a thousand years. Creeping through archways and tunnels I came to a central building. There was a beautiful, hexagonal room with a floor of soft-colored, rubbed stone and a big, central, though broken, skylight. The place enchanted me, and I at once set about enlisting my friends as cleaning-men and renovators.

Akiva Govrin, who later became Minister of Tourism in the Israeli Government, volunteered to wash the floors, and others now in high, official positions repaired the roof and whitewashed the walls. Asaf Goor-Grasovsky then in the agricultural department of the Mandatory Government, helped me set up a line of cans containing plants, leading from the Jaffa Gate to the exhibition hall of the Citadel. Invitations were printed in the three official languages of English, Hebrew and Arabic, and I was elated by the thought that I was pioneering good relations between the three peoples through the sacred power of art.

The exhibition made a great stir; my friends and the general public were enthusiastic, although Sir Herbert Samuel, the High Commissioner, declared that the paintings were "too revolutionary" to be hung in the Citadel. On the other hand, Sir Ronald Storrs was an admirer of my work and to encourage the purchase of paintings by officials, he himself was the first to acquire a canvas. Many of the paintings and drawings were sold, mostly to people of European background who were employed by the government or by the Zionist Mission.

Reviews were enthusiastic and I was greatly encouraged by the remarkably cordial response of the public. At that time there were few artists in Israel and we formed a closely knit group. The reception given to my exhibition was the impetus for the creation of the Palestine Association of Painters and Sculptors, which, in a vastly enlarged form, is still active today.

THE GLORY OF GALILEE 1965/66 *oil on canvas* collection, The Knesset, Jerusalem

Although the invitations has been printed in Arabic, I can remember seeing only one Arab at the exhibition. He was a sheik from Bethlehem who came twice with his beautiful sixteen-year-old daughter, dressed in a traditional embroidered robe. He was under the impression that an exhibition was a place where rich gentlemen would come and that he would be able to dispose of his daughter at a good price.

My Jerusalem exhibition was followed by one in Tel Aviv, at the Herzlia Gymnasium (high school), the only large building in the town. This was visited by crowds of young people who expressed their appreciation with considerable rowdiness.

The two cities of Jerusalem and Tel Aviv were completely different from one another not only in physical aspects but in character. It was difficult to believe they were situated but a small distance from one another. Jerusalem, with its stone buildings, old and new, and its population, made up mainly of government employees and officials and the various Zionist bodies, had nothing in common with the happy-go-lucky, uninhibited "worker" population of Tel Aviv. Tel Aviv resembled a market place; the buildings had a provisional look, but the population was alive, alert and striving to do its utmost for the development not only of a home but of a people. No visitor or tourist on a short stay could possibly grasp what Tel Aviv meant for the new country. One had to live there and be part of its life to feel the energy and vitality that were creating the future characteristics of the Jewish homeland.

Tel Aviv was—and still is—a noisy city. It even then pulsated with vigor. The most peculiar and interesting aspect was the singing and dancing in the streets. The energies of the young people found their outlet in group singing and dancing, even after a hard day's work in the heat. There were no special places of entertainment; girls and boys met in the streets or down on the beach and quite spontaneously linked arms to dance a *hora* or stood together in groups to sing the new songs that spoke of the country and its landscape. In this relaxed atmosphere, I felt free of worries. I loved to visit the Galilee villages or spend time in the picturesque city of the Cabala, Safed, which was the coolest spot in the country in the heat of summer. Low-lying Tiberias I loved too, with the lake of Kinneret reflecting the sky and the purples and pinks of the hills of Moab on the farther side.

MIMOSA AND BLACK IRIS 1961 *oil on canvas* 40 × 30 collection, Sir Isaac and Lady Wolfson, London

After I had been back in Palestine for two years, had held two exhibitions and collected together a number of works, I began to feel a longing for change. I wanted to show my paintings to a more sophisticated audience and to hear trenchant criticism or well-informed appreciation from connoisseurs.

Very generously, friends came to my aid with loans of five pounds each, and when I had a capital of fifty pounds, I packed my cases and set out for Europe.

My aim was Paris, but my old circle in Bucharest clamored for an exhibition, and so it was to Rumania that I initially found my way. The exhibition there again brought highly favorable reviews and remarks on "the astonishing new style" of my paintings. Sales, however, were few. During my stay I designed the decor for performances of the Vilna Troupe, an excellent group of Yiddish actors then in Bucharest. I especially remember my stage designs for the Ossip Dimoff play, *The Singer of His Sadness*, in which a new actor, Joseph Buloff, had the leading role. He has since become famous.

The designing of the sets entailed much thought and time, as the means were very limited. Many things had not been carried out the way I wanted. I was afraid my decor would be a failure and I left for Paris without waiting for the opening. But happily the play became one of the outstanding successes of the troupe; Buloff was acclaimed for his performance and my work also received much praise.

When I arrived in Paris at the end of 1924, I was again without a single friend to whom I could turn. But Paris, with all the opportunities it held out for an artist, had always attracted me, and I let myself be guided by my instincts. My first step was to find a place to live and to store my paintings. With the money loaned me by my friends in Palestine, I had the means to rent a proper studio.

I looked forward to living in Montmartre, the dream of every young artist, so that I could have a chance to meet other artists and to establish a "human contact" with Paris. As I walked along the streets looking for a "*Chambre à Louer*" sign, chance brought me to the Rue Trézel. In the window of a house I saw a notice of a room to let, and since the neighborhood made a friendly impression on me, I went in. The woman who rented me the room was a milliner, and a number of hats were exhibited on stands in the window. Naturally, I took it for granted that if she let me the room,

she would remove the hats. But not at all! Day after day the hats remained where they were, and every now and again the hatmaker would come into my room—most of the time without knocking but always with a smile—and remove a hat or bring back another. I didn't have the courage to ask her to take the hats away, nor did I want the bother of looking for another place to live, so I stayed, trying to get used to living in a sort of millinery shop while trying to make the room suitable to work in.

Most of my time I spent visiting museums, the Louvre and the Luxembourg, and the galleries. Or I just walked through the streets and boulevards, wondering how I would ever manage to hold an exhibition in Paris or achieve anything at all in this great, glorious city. One day while strolling along, I met an acquaintance from Tel Aviv who told me that that very evening there was to be a party in the home of a young American couple, and he invited me to come along. The host was a gifted writer, Marvin Lowenthal, who, with his wife Sylvia, had come from New York to Paris for a few years' stay, a move which at that time was considered almost essential for a serious American writer. I was delighted to accept the invitation and to have a chance to be with people.

That same day the *vernissage* of the Salon d'Automne took place, and I spent a long time at the exhibition. Among the works which particularly impressed me was a large, plaster head which was very bold and expressive in form. The catalogue said it was a "Portrait of the Artist Laboureur," by Orloff. I liked the piece enormously, and the name of the artist remained in my mind. That evening at the Lowenthals, whose apartment in a charming old house on the banks of the Seine reflected their culture and taste, there were many young people, mostly writers, painters and musicians. Among the people to whom I was introduced was a portly woman by the name of Orloff, who was sitting in a corner. I remarked what a strange coincidence it was that in one day I should twice encounter the name of Orloff, not a common one, and I told her how much I had been impressed by a portrait bust sculpted by a Russian named Orloff.

To my amazement, Mme. Orloff told me that she was the creator of the head, that she was Russian by origin but had come from Palestine and was now living in Paris. This was one of those chance meetings, that came to profoundly enrich my life. Chana Orloff was gratified to receive a compliment, especially from an unknown admirer, and we at once became good friends—a relationship that lasted over forty years. She asked me to come to her studio in the Rue d'Assa. She thought she would like to do a head of me.

The visit to Orloff's studio a few days later was my first real introduction to the life of an artist in Paris. It was a large room in a courtyard, surrounded by other studios. One corner of her room was reserved for the kitchen; another corner, concealed by a curtain, served as a bedroom; the rest was the sculpture studio.

Chana was young and full of energy. First she put a big pot of *borsht* on the stove and then started preparing the clay for my bust. She was a

LANDSCAPE NEAR SAFED   1958/63   *oil on canvas*   38 × 62   collection, Mr. and Mrs. W. B. Herman, Toronto

formidable worker and a remarkable person. She got the clay ready, then jumped up to see how the *borsht* was getting on. Occasionally she went behind the curtain, and I realized there was a child there who, as I learned later, was ill.

But nothing seemed to depress Chana's spirit, which reminded me of the spirit of Tel Aviv itself, vigorous and alive. She spoke fluent Hebrew and there was always one particular song on her lips, *El Yivneh Hagalil* (God Will Build the Galilee). She worked furiously on the bust and by the afternoon I saw my head taking shape, looking like the Negus of Abyssinia. But it was a fine piece of work and I liked it from the start.

My friendship with Chana Orloff gave me insight into the art world of Montparnasse and the manner in which exhibitions came to be arranged.

Later, through her, I received an invitation from the well-known poet and writer, Edmond Fleg. I had already read some of his works and felt privileged to be invited to his home. He and his gracious wife Madeleine lived in a beautiful apartment on the Ile Saint Louis, the Seine on one side and Notre Dame on the other. In their home I felt that I was in the heart of Paris. This, I mused, is what I had read about in Balzac, Anatole France, Baudelaire and Hugo.

There was a group of distinguished guests at the Flegs, and I seemed to be "the curiosity of the moment," an artist from the remote Holy Land about which they actually knew very little. They were aware only that certain Jews were trying to create a new homeland there and that they spoke a language which had existed for some two thousand years but only as the tongue of the Bible.

I told many stories of the "revival" of the Jewish people. I felt inspired that evening, and in that wonderful home, surrounded by friendly, sympathetic people, all the feelings that had accumulated inside me during my years of struggle and loneliness, and the love I had for the hot, sandy country of Palestine, came pouring out of me in a torrent of words.

Some days prior to my visit to the Flegs' home, the Yiddish Granovsky Theatre from Russia had come to Paris, and I never missed any of their performances. Headed by the great actor, Michoels, they were an unusual body of fine artists. That evening at Edmond Fleg's, I talked about this theatre, especially about a play called *The Travels of Benjamin the Third*, a fantastic, mystical Jewish folklore tale. It was not easy for me to explain to these Frenchmen of high intellectual attainments what it was that made this play about a poor Jew and his aspirations so great, and to make clear to them how wonderfully the actors had interpreted this theme. But among those present that evening were two ladies, Mme. Clemenceau, wife of the great statesman, and Mme. Bernheim, of the great art dealer's family, who appeared to be fascinated by my stories. They expressed a desire to see this phenomenal theatrical company and asked that I accompany them and explain the play.

A date was set, and in the company of these two ladies I again enjoyed *The Travels of Benjamin the Third*, but sitting this time in a box of the grand circle. I was pleased to see that both of them were deeply impressed.

After the performance, Mme. Bernheim said that she would like to see my paintings. On the appointed day, she arrived at the Rue Trézel in her big limousine, which made a great impression not only on my land-lady but on the whole street. Mme. Bernheim could not keep a smile off her face as she watched my landlady rush into my room to change the hats in the window and the way in which I had to pull my paintings out from under the bed, not having any other place to keep them.

After looking at my work, she went to the telephone to call someone. I learned later that he was André Schoeller, a gallery owner with a great reputation in the art world. He came over almost at once and was enthusiastic enough about my work to have a number of canvases taken immediately to his gallery. He asked me to have lunch with him in a few days so that he could arrange for some of the press to meet me. I could hardly believe what was happening! Mme. Bernheim and M. Schoeller sitting in my room and my paintings being taken over to the gallery! So many things were taking place and at such speed.

I could not wait to rush over to Chana Orloff and tell her the news, and she too could not believe her ears.

"This calls for a celebration at the Rotonde," she said, and off we went. Thus I began to meet those painters about whom I had only read or whose names I had seen in catalogues: Pascin, Soutine, Kisling, Derain. I had a strong feeling that I must guard myself in case I be submerged in the sea of French art life. For in my ears I again heard the call of the Land of Israel and my father's singing of *Hallelujah*.

At the exhibition the paintings I showed had no connection with any of the current French schools or trends and were seen as a personal and individual expression of an artist from Palestine. Important articles appeared in the press, one of which was a full page in *Excelsior* with criticism by Louis Vauxcelles and photographs of my work. All the reviews were highly laudatory and one particularly pleased me, for the critic wrote: "With the art of Rubin a new style has been born, not a Jewish style, but a Hebrew style." These words gave me great encouragement and showed me that I was on the right road.

The French Government acquired a painting, and there were many other sales, mostly to people from America and Germany. At the end of the exhibition, M. Schoeller told me that he was prepared to take all of my paintings, and proposed that I sign a five-year agreement with him. The conditions were that I should stay in Paris, continue to paint in the same style, and produce a specific number of works of certain dimensions.

I should have been flattered, but, instead, a chill gripped my heart. It seemed to me that if I accepted this proposal it would mean the end of all my dreams. I would have to stay in Paris, produce paintings which should be not too big nor too small.

When I heard my patron speak of paintings in specific sizes and quantities I had a strong feeling of disillusionment. All my friends congratulated me on my success but I could not rid myself of a great sadness. And so I decided I had better leave Paris as soon as possible.

Not being able to leave Paris immediately, I stayed another few months to reap the fruits of my success. My life revolved around Montparnasse, where at café tables I met the notables of the art world. It was the period when French galleries were exploding with the paintings of such artists as Picasso, Matisse, Derain, Vlaminck. An excitement of "liberated art" permeated the air, and although it was true that I was participating in the animated spirit of the day, inwardly I felt it was all really strange to me. It was not my world. Frequent visits to the studios of Pascin and Kisling and others proved to me that their way of life, in spite of all their artistic achievements, could never replace my humble dreams and desires, which were not merely to paint and live the life of an artist, but to do so in Palestine, among my own people who were seeking to build a new, free way of life.

As the time approached for my departure, many friends tried to dissuade me from leaving. Only that great soul, Edmond Fleg, who was the personification of idealism and goodness, gave me the courage to hold fast to my decision. He alone was able to understand my inward longings. And although I had found a second home in the Fleg household, I left Paris for the same reason I had left New York after my first exhibition there: the urge to shape my life in accordance with my innermost feelings, the feelings I had for my people, my family, my country—Palestine. I wanted to express these feelings in my work. When I had left America, I felt I must escape from the pressures exerted by the impact of the huge buildings and the way of life which I realized was not mine. Now I was leaving Paris because I felt I must escape from the pressures imposed by French culture and French tradition. Beautiful and invigorating as they were, I would not allow them to envelop me.

In October, 1926, I wrote a brief essay for the *Menorah Journal*, at the suggestion of my friend, Marvin Lowenthal. In it I expressed in simple terms what I felt:

> Here in Jerusalem, Tel Aviv, Haifa and Tiberias I feel myself reborn. Only here do I feel that life and nature are mine. The grey clouds of Europe have disappeared. My sufferings and the war too are ended. All is sunshine, clear light and happy, creative work. As the desert revives and blooms under the hands of the pioneers, so do I feel awakening in me all the latent energies . . .
> I live with simple people, I walk the old Galilean roads and ride on horseback from Ir Ganim to Tel Aviv with milkmen and farmers. The horizon has broad, curved lines. The air is clear and transparent and the perspective of European atmosphere no longer deforms nature for me. Men here are simple dreamers. Life is full of surprises for them. Everything is new and their wide-open eyes regard the world with wonderment. I have pitched my tent on these ancient hills and my desire is to tie together the ends of the thread that history has broken.

Return to Palestine

Full of the impetus to work, I went back to Tel Aviv. With the funds that still remained from my Paris stay, I could afford to take a larger apartment in one of the new houses which had been built with a view of the Mediterranean. Then I sent money to Falticeni urging my aged parents and a younger sister to come and join me. I thought I could give my father no greater pleasure than to bring him to Palestine and let his eyes bathe in the reality of his dreams. But he did not make the trip, for he died just about at the time when my letter arrived. My mother and sister were able to come, and with their arrival I felt that my last ties with Europe had been broken and that I was now firmly settled in Palestine.

The year 1926 was one of my most productive periods. It was then that I painted the three big canvases: "The Dancers of Meron," "Portrait of Achad Ha'am," and "Jews of Jerusalem." All of my paintings of that period were imbued with the joy of living. Although I kept my colors low-keyed and pale, the designs were harmonious, and the eyes of the figures in my canvases were wide open to the future.

It was at about this time that the great poet, Chaim Nachman Bialik arrived in Palestine, and I was fortunate to be able to enjoy a warm friendship with him. After days spent in work came evenings of wonderful talk with Bialik. He was both wise and witty, and the hours spent in his company were for me like the rays of a lighthouse to men lost at sea.

Since there were then no galleries or museums in Tel Aviv, I held an exhibition in a private home. The introduction to the catalogue was written by Bialik. It was, as far as I know, the only article on art ever written by the great poet. It gave me a feeling of elation and confidence to receive recognition from the community and to read Bialik's exalted words. His appearance on the country's scene was a real inspiration to me and his conversation and writings gave me the spiritual support I needed.

My exhibition proved also a material success, with some paintings sold to foreigners as well as local citizens. Although I now had my mother and sister to support I no longer felt the strain of financial need. And now life was pleasanter in other ways, for Tel Aviv had started to evolve its own little "Montparnasse," with special cafés where artists, writers and theatre people met and passed lively evenings in discussion and song.

But after about eighteen months I returned to Paris, anxious to prove to my colleagues there that from the standpoint of my artistic development I had been right to go to Palestine. I had a happy reunion with my Parisian friends, and Chana Orloff and Kisling were particularly enthusiastic when they saw the work I had brought with me.

GOING TO THE MARKET 1960 *pen, ink and pastel* private collection, New York

AFTER THE STORM 1965 *oil on canvas* 36 × 29 collection of the artist

וְהִנֵּה רֶכֶב־אֵשׁ
וְסוּסֵי־אֵשׁ
וַיַּעַל אֵלִיָּהוּ
בַּסְעָרָה הַשָּׁמָיִם

rubin 1967

I was thinking of another exhibition, but I did not want to apply to Schoeller again, as I felt I had let him down when I left France earlier. I found a comfortable studio in Montparnasse, which I leased from an absentee artist. At first life went along pleasantly and easily, but I soon found it almost impossible to do any work, for the anxiety of trying to arrange an exhibition so that I could return as soon as possible to Palestine weighed on me. And I had great difficulty in finding a gallery. By chance I visited an exhibition by Vlaminck at the Druet Gallery in the Rue Royale. I was very impressed and felt it would be a great thing if I could have an exhibition there. So I made a point of meeting the gallery director, M. Atis. He was a most agreeable person and a fine connoisseur, and after a friendly chat he politely agreed to come to my studio and look at the paintings I had brought from Palestine. I felt that he had accepted my invitation only out of courtesy, but when he came to my studio, to my great satisfaction he studied my work very attentively. He said that he was happy to see a young artist who showed "so much love for his people and so much joy of living."

He perceived Hebraic influences in my paintings and expressed his pleasure at finding a young painter who "had learned the lessons of French art but yet was not trying to follow this or that fashionable trend."

I was very pleased to hear his remarks, as I had always been afraid of being isolated. I well realized that in the last fifteen or twenty years numerous movements had made their appearance in the art world: the *fauves*, the cubists, the expressionists, the futurists, all tearing like meteors across the sky of art. These words of appreciation from such a connoisseur as M. Atis reminded me of similar remarks that Alfred Stieglitz had made to me years ago in New York.

On the spot, M. Atis phoned his wife to come and join him in my studio, and her reaction was equally favorable. The following day I went to the gallery and a date for the exhibition, a month later, was set.

The rooms of the Druet Gallery were spacious and well-lit and formed a fine background for my large collection of paintings. The press and my artist friends received the show very well, but there were few sales. I tried to analyze the reasons for the lack of purchasers: perhaps my way of painting had changed in the last few years and was no longer attractive to collectors. On the other hand, I felt that I was on the right path. I had

not deliberately changed my style and such changes as had come about were instinctive.

Some of my friends who had knowledge of the technicalities of art dealing in Paris explained that the financial failure was not due to artistic reasons. It was simply because this time I didn't have the dynamic support of the Bernheim-Schoeller team.

Still, I had to follow my instincts, which told me that the manner in which art dealers operated was not for me. And Paris was beautiful, my exhibition gratified me personally, my circle of friends liked the paintings, and M. Atis still continued to express his admiration. So I cannot truly say that I was unhappy. But I felt somewhat guilty, for I realized that from my meager sales, M. Atis could not even hope to cover his expenses on such a big show.

Then, early one summer morning, something unexpected occurred: I had a visit from an art critic whom I had met in New York in 1921 and who had written a complimentary review of my work. His name was Dr. Christian Brinton. He had obtained my address from a London reviewer who had written about my last Paris show. Dr. Brinton told me that the show had found favorable echoes in the American as well as the English press and he was convinced that I should have another New York exhibition after my Paris success.

I told him that although the exhibition could be considered a success from the critical standpoint, it had not been financially successful. And to go to New York was a costly business which I could not afford. He then said that he would try to get in touch with a gallery director he knew, George Hellman. Thereupon, he sat down and wrote an extremely favorable letter to Mr. Hellman, enclosing some photographs of my work. Then he left, and to this day I have never seen Dr. Brinton again, but his letter was to have an effect in due time.

One afternoon, while sitting on the terrace of the Coupole, I ran into an American acquaintance whom I had previously met in Palestine, Alex Lamport. We started to talk and I told him, among other things, that I expected to return to Palestine soon, although an American art critic had proposed that I have a New York exhibition. I said that although I would have liked to have seen New York again, and especially my old friend, Alfred Stieglitz, I knew from experience that I could not expect too much. Furthermore, I did not have the money to get to America. To my astonishment, Alex Lamport took out his checkbook and wrote a check for a substantial amount. He handed it to me with the words, "You should go. We'll all be delighted to have you in New York. And you can repay me after the exhibition."

I was deeply touched by this generosity, especially since it was solely a friendly impulse; Mr. Lamport was not particularly interested in art.

The money burned a hole in my pocket but I did not want to set out

on another American adventure before hearing from the New York dealer. At last a letter came from Mr. Hellman.

He wrote that although the reviews and photographs impressed him, he could not offer me an exhibition as he had just closed his gallery for good and had no connections with any other established gallery. Although I was disappointed, the adverse news, instead of influencing me to return to Palestine, rather determined me to make the visit to New York anyway. "It's a challenge and I am going to accept it," I said to myself.

I began preparations for the trip. Again I would be in New York on my own, but this time I would at least have funds to support myself for a few months. The future I would leave to my luck and the power of my paintings.

FAMILY AT REST   1963   *pen, ink and pastel*   private collection, Paris △

◁ THE BIG BOUQUET   1964   *oil on canvas*   46 × 35   collection, Mr. Irving Geist, New York

MIMOSA 1961 *oil on canvas* 46 × 35 collection, Israel Museum, Jerusalem

New York Again

I arrived in New York on a splendid May day with a clear blue sky overhead. This time it seemed to me that the skyscrapers directed their thousands of eyes at the incoming ships with a more friendly glance. Now that I knew English better the city was no longer so strange to me, and with some money at my disposal I could walk down the gangplank with a confident air. I soon found a wonderful place to live, a studio apartment at 90 West 40th Street. It was called, without my being aware of it, the Beaux Arts Apartments. There was a good restaurant in the basement and my windows opened on to the park where the New York Public Library stood. Everything looked rosy to me. The receptionist always had a warm smile for me and it seemed as if the people I saw in the street were also in a high-spirited, optimistic mood. I could not imagine how such a change had come about in a few years.

Later I understood. This was 1928, the height of prosperity. The last time I had been in New York, arriving at the end of 1920, there still remained something of the World War I slump.

My paintings had not yet arrived from Paris and I was free as a bird for the time being. I spent all my time at the Metropolitan Museum and other galleries or just walking about Central Park, enjoying the sunshine. But the gay spring mood did not last long. All too soon New York became humid and hot, and living there started to be disagreeable.

As I walked along Fifth Avenue one day, a car drew up to the curb and an old acquaintance from my previous visit called to me. He seemed pleased to see me and after a short talk invited me to come and stay with him and his family at Lake Placid. Mr. Stone, my acquaintance, was now a wealthy businessman and I remembered that his family were sympathetic, intelligent people. The invitation was a godsend, for the heat of New York was torrid; even Palestine's summers were more bearable. I packed my working materials and promised myself to make up for lost time.

Lake Placid was a delightful place. A beautiful room and studio over the garage were placed at my disposal. It was the first time in my life that I had ever gone on a real vacation. One of the first people I met at the Stones' home was Jascha Heifetz, the violinist, who was a friend of the family. He was young, dashing, with a quick though somewhat caustic wit. He was vacationing with his family as well as giving concerts in the

Overleaf: ROAD TO SAFED   1960   *oil on canvas*   24 × 36   private collection, Chicago

vicinity. I was greatly taken with him and deeply impressed by his confidence in his own talent. It was like a dose of good medicine to me, for I was always worried, insecure and riddled by self-doubt. My friendship with Heifetz has continued till this day, and some of my happiest moments have been passed listening to his superb playing.

Mr. Stone's youngest daughter had been married a few years previously to a physician, and the new couple were both passionate lovers of painting and sculpture. They had an adorable little girl of about three and I painted her portrait in a pink nightgown, playing with a doll. I painted it in the direct, primitive manner which was characteristic of my work at that time; Mr. Stone bought it at once.

Before leaving New York for Lake Placid, I had not telephoned either George Hellman or Alfred Stieglitz. Since Mr. Hellman had written that he no longer had any connections with art galleries, I took his reply as a sign that he did not wish to be bothered with me. As for Stieglitz, while he had previously been so kind to me and had given me such encouragement, he had not replied to any of my letters. So I assumed he too had forgotten me.

At Lake Placid, however, in talking about the possibility of an exhibition, George Hellman's name came up in the conversation. I learned that he was vacationing nearby, at his family home on Saranac Lake. I was urged to overcome my shyness and to telephone him. I did so, and Mr. Hellman most cordially said that he would come over to Lake Placid to see me. When he came I liked him immediately. He was distinguished in manner and appearance—tall, thin, with a little pointed beard and twinkling blue eyes. He was intrigued by my work and invited me to visit his home in Saranac to meet his mother. She was an elderly, nineteenth century type lady, who spoke beautiful French and could recite poems by Valery and Mallarmé by heart. We chatted in French together, and later she gave a dinner in my honor, inviting friends living around the lake. These included members of the Lewisohn, Lehman, and Seligman families, who represented the aristocracy of the Jewish community at that time.

After dinner, all the guests wanted to hear about Palestine. To them it was as if I were talking about another planet, but they listened intently and asked many questions. At one point, Mr. Hellman's mother made what I took to be a very typical American remark: "Mr. Rubin, please be careful how you answer. Around the table are sitting 400 million dollars."

This designation in terms of money was no longer strange to me, as newspaper headlines often ran, "Five Million Dollar Fire," or "Ten Million Dollar Strike."

The month at Lake Placid provided a most enjoyable break. I did a certain amount of painting but very few landscapes. Although the area was indeed beautiful, it was not my type of landscape. I had never seen such intense greens, blues or blacks. In Palestine, the strong sunlight drains away the color; the air is thin and transparent and colors are bluish or rosy, with traces of ochre and orange.

FISHERMAN IN GALILEE 1959 *oil on canvas* 29 × 36 collection, Mr. and Mrs. Philip J. Levin, New York

The time I spent in the company of these pleasant, understanding people at Lake Placid and Saranac produced a great change in my outlook on life. For so many years I had been very much alone, morose, with few interludes of gaiety or relaxation, always trying to improve my knowledge, and with work the uppermost thought in my mind. But here I ate rich foods and tasted champagne for the first time.

Mr. Hellman was most encouraging and said that when he returned to New York he would come and see my other paintings. He would even look into the possibilities of an exhibition. My paintings arrived shortly after I got back to New York and as I looked at them in my studio—my Galilee landscapes, my Jerusalem scenes, my fishermen and flute players—I realized that they were far more sophisticated in execution and varied in texture than my work of eight years ago. But I wondered how they would be received by New Yorkers living in skyscrapers, hurrying to business and happy to live in a modern and prosperous land.

But my fears were soon lessened. The Stones were the first to come to my studio and they acquired a number of canvases. My financial difficulties were now lightened and I was in a position to repay the loan received from Alex Lamport. I could begin to work again with a free mind.

George Hellman also came to inspect the paintings and reacted very favorably. He said that he would try and make some contacts in the art world on my behalf and it was not too long before he brought me the good news that I could have an exhibition at the Guarino Gallery, which had taken over his old premises. He also introduced me to collectors, arranging a meeting with the late Mme. Helena Rubinstein, the cosmetics queen and art lover. John Erskine, author of the bestseller, *Helen of Troy*, was also present, and the meeting resulted both in sales and lasting friendships.

All these events imbued me with a tremendous drive to work, and many paintings of New York scenes appeared in my studio during this period. The general opinion was that these works were good, but I was not satisfied with them and, like my Lake Placid landscapes, I decided never to show them publicly. Good or bad, they were not "me," as were my Palestine landscapes.

Some time later Mr. Hellman told me that he was trying to arrange for the famous Knoedler Gallery to exhibit my works at the opening of their new gallery in Chicago. The director, Mr. Messmore, came to my studio and, after several talks with Mr. Hellman, chose twelve paintings which were to be sent to Knoedler's New York gallery for appraisal.

The twelve paintings selected were taken off to Knoedler's in their special van, but at the end of the week the paintings were returned and the deal never came through. The real reason I did not learn at the time; but I later heard it had to do with the matter of Mr. Hellman's commission. The failure of the project did not unduly depress me, even though I knew what it would have meant for my future to have the prestige of being represented at that time by Knoedler's. But I remembered that when

ORIENTALE 1955 *oil on canvas* $35\frac{1}{2} \times 32$ collection, Mr. and Mrs. Harold Weill, New York

LA PECHE MIRACULEUSE 1966 *tapestry* 106 × 75 collection, Mr. and Mrs. Bernard Bloomfield, Montreal
collection, Mr. and Mrs. Melvin Gelman, Washington, D.C.
collection, Mr. and Mrs. W. B. Herman, Toronto

Andre Schoeller in Paris had wanted to handle my work, I had rejected the plan. There was something in my character which always revolted against being "handled" and given instructions. The easy life was not for me. I wished to fight alone and make my own way. It was Hellman who was really disappointed and I had to console him.

The exhibition I ultimately had at the Guarino Gallery was beautifully shown and George Hellman wrote a fine introduction to the catalogue. The notices were extremely favorable. One of the first people to be interested in the paintings was Otto H. Kahn, a well-known patron of the arts, with whom I made friends. Many others followed his example.

The winter of 1928 was a happy and contented time for me, unlike anything I had known before. I began to get to know the Americans and was captivated by their humor, their easy friendliness and their amazing capacity for "getting things done." But by the beginning of 1929, I decided that the time had come for me to return to Palestine. I was now in a position to do what I had always dreamed of ever since I first went to Palestine: to buy some land and plant an orange grove.

Wanting my return trip to be a restful holiday, I took passage on the *Mauretania*, which was going to make a Mediterranean cruise and call at a number of ports, arriving in Palestine after twenty-two days at sea. For the first time in my life I booked a first-class cabin and bought some presentable luggage. No more bundles tied up in string! This cruise was to become the most fateful journey of my life.

△ VISIT OF THE ANGELS 1963 *drawing, pen and ink* private collection, New York

ABRAHAM AND THE THREE ANGELS 1965 *oil on canvas* 76 × 51 collection of the artist ▷

I Meet My Future Wife

I decided that I would spend the twenty-two days lolling in a deck chair and reading. But the day after the ship sailed, as I was sitting on deck, I saw a girl walking along wearing what was then known as the "college girl's raccoon coat." She attracted me from the moment I laid eyes on her.

I put down the book I was reading and went over to her. She was very young, but what I principally noticed were her large, sea-colored eyes. I introduced myself to her with the name "Rubin," which meant nothing to her, and she told me that her name was Esther Davis, which meant nothing to me. I continued to walk along the deck with her and accompanied her to the purser's office to send off some letters. She told me she was traveling with a group of students, third class. I interrupted her to ask her to marry me. How I dared make such a proposal after an acquaintance of a few minutes, I do not know. But ask her I did. She looked shocked, made no reply, then walked away. But at least I knew her name and where she was to be found.

At that point began a cruise courtship. Daily I sent flowers and invitations. All I wanted was to be with Esther Davis. I learned from her that she had won a national oratorical contest in New York for which the prize was a trip to Palestine and back. Prior to her departure she had appeared on the radio to receive her award and the speaker who introduced her had read a poem which referred to the "beautiful Shulamith," comparing Esther to the girl of the poem. When she told me what the lines were I was stunned, for I realized that they were from a poem I had written in Yiddish many years ago, which had later been published. "Come, Shulamith, to the fields with me. Come to the mountains with me, Shulamith."

I looked upon this coincidence as a happy omen for my future. The cruise gave us an opportunity to become well acquainted with each other, and giving no more thought to my first-class ticket, I spent the rest of my time in third class.

On a cheerful day in March, 1929, we arrived in Haifa. Esther remained there, where a big reception was to be arranged by the Young Judea organization which had given her the prize, and I went back to my home in Tel Aviv. She had given me no answer to my several proposals of marriage and so my mood was rather gloomy, although she did promise to meet me in Tel Aviv shortly afterwards.

ESTHER 1943 *oil on canvas* 26 × 20 Sam Lewisohn collection, New York

After more than a year abroad I was glad to be back in Tel Aviv. The beautiful spring days, the clear Palestinian sky delighted me. My exhibitions in Paris and New York had furnished me with funds and I was awaiting Esther's arrival. Tel Aviv was in the throes of preparations for a huge Purim carnival and I was called in to help as I always had for various celebrations. A few days after my return to Tel Aviv, I saw Esther standing in front of a photographer's window where my portrait was displayed. As I watched her I said to myself, "This time I won't let you get away again."

As I showed her around the city, her youthful, enthusiastic response to all that she saw convinced me that I had at last found the partner for whom I had been waiting all my life. We literally blazed through the explosive days of the carnival in a state of exaltation. Already Tel Aviv and Palestine were becoming for Esther the same sort of "necessity" they were for me. There was no longer any doubt of our continuing together. She gave up the idea of returning to the United States with the group with which she had come to Palestine, and I tried to find some work for her which would utilize her fine command of English.

The year was 1929. My American success and the realization that I would be able to build a life with Esther gave me a new, optimistic attitude which I had never known before. The mere thought of a real home filled me with happiness. No longer a movable tent but a permanent home.

I bought a piece of land in the vicinity of Tel Aviv and had it prepared for planting an orange grove. Then I began to design a studio which would be erected on the highest part of the land. I was following the Biblical injunction: "Plant yourself a tree and build your house in its shade." I still remember clearly the day the planting was started, when we found water after digging only a few meters under the ground, and the wonderful moment when the water started to gush out, inundating the surrounding land.

But the heat of summer was to bring trouble with it: the bloodshed and violence of Arab riots. The peaceful haven that I had just started to build seemed on the verge of collapse. But with Esther at my side I had the feeling that everything would turn out for the best.

Toward the end of 1929 my painting again underwent a great change. Till then the larger part of my work had consisted of figure compositions in a serene, primitive setting. Now my new life and my hopes for the future made me look more closely at the actual realities round me: the landscape, the fruit and flowers of the country. Until that time I had not painted landscapes proper but rather had created formalized, even idealized statements that were not tied to any specific time. In my paintings, Jerusalem, Tiberias, Safed, Jaffa, always appeared colored by my imagination. The stony walls of Jerusalem, the dreaming sea of Galilee or mystical Safed were an expression of qualities I felt they had had long ago but had lost. But suddenly the landscape and flowers became a living reality for me. I can recall exactly when this happened to me. I was on my way to Jeru-

DAVID 1948 *oil on canvas* 12 × 10½ collection, Mr. and Mrs. David Rubin, Caesarea

ARIELLA   1956   *oil on canvas*   12 × 10½   collection, Mr. and Mrs. M. Aharonee, Rome

salem with Esther on one of our many trips together. We approached the beautiful village of Abu Ghosh, surrounded by ancient olive trees. I stopped the car and stood amazed, for I saw the countryside in a completely different way than I ever had before. It seemed to me that the landscape and its olive trees were leaning toward me, embracing me. The colors, the light, the shimmering atmosphere in which the landscape seemed to breathe and live—it was like a revelation. I took out my sketchbook and started to draw, making notes of colors I had never noticed before. I remembered that a biography of Van Gogh which I had read said that he made sketches of landscapes, noting down the different colors with descriptive remarks about them. At the time I had thought, what is the use of putting down in words "brownish ochre" or "ultramarine blue"? But when I started to do the same thing, I realized that I was tremendously moved by emotion and yet not able to sit down and paint at once what was before me, so that these notes helped liberate my spirit from the obsession of the scene. In my studio afterward, I would cover many canvases, attempting to recapture my feelings at the moment when I "discovered" the beauty of the natural landscape. Continually I saw in my mind's eye the greens, the greys, the ochres of the hillsides, the blue of the sky and the silver shimmering of the olive trees that created a subtle symphony of color. It was never my way to look for or choose a subject; it was always as if the subject chose and took hold of *me*, so that I could not escape from it until I had set it down. This fact also explains why I have never allowed "theories" to interfere with my instincts about painting. I have always felt intuitively what I should do and I did it.

The British Government sent a Commission of Enquiry to look into the causes of the Arab riots of 1929 and it was with this Commission that Esther got her first job. She made many trips with them to distant parts of the country and used to tell me her impressions of the varied landscapes. The countryside was impressive but the food was not, and on one of these occasions she contracted typhus. I was afraid that her illness would make her homesick for her family and America and that her desire to remain in Palestine would weaken. But on the contrary, when she recovered she was even more convinced that she wanted to make her life in Palestine with me. So we finalized our marriage plans and in 1930, a year after her arrival and after another Purim carnival in Tel Aviv, we were married in a ceremony on the roof of my home in the presence of a few friends who came straight from the Purim dancing and merrymaking. At eight o'clock in the morning I said goodbye to my family and with my beloved Esther went to Egypt, invited by the Baron de Menasce to spend a few weeks of our honeymoon there. Then we went on to Paris, London and New York. Without telling Esther, I had accepted an offer for an exhibition at the Arthur Tooth Gallery in London.

The visit to Egypt was my second, and now I had an opportunity to see Upper Egypt and all the amazing treasures of the Pharaohs. Visting the places mentioned in the Bible kindled my imagination; the towering figure of Moses and the Exodus from Egypt became so real to me that there were moments when I felt that I had actually lived at that period in a previous existence. Surely once I was a slave in the land of Egypt and had helped to build the pyramids and inscribe the hieroglyphics on the pillars.

After our weeks in this enchanted, ancient place I took Esther to Paris. I wanted her to see the places where sixteen years previously I had wandered as a lonely, yearning young man. But now every day was a holiday. I took Esther to see the hotel on the Rue des Ecoles where I had lived, the restaurant on the Rue Ticquetonne which, I understood, was still offering drunkards a free meal if they would drink a bottle of milk with it, the Ecole des Beaux Arts on the Rue Bonaparte and, of course, the wonderful museums with their art treasures. It was spring, time of enchantment, and I loved to watch the delight on my companion's expressive face and to see her amusement and interest in the lively scenes at the Montparnasse cafés. We lived in a dream but reality was just ahead, for we had to go on to London where my paintings had already arrived.

My good friend Dudley Tooth and the gallery officials made my exhibition a very pleasant one. The writer Louis Golding let us have his home in London while he went off to Europe. He even left us his servant so that we lived in a state of unaccustomed comfort. The English friends we had made in Palestine were most gracious: Israel Sieff and his sprightly wife Becky kept open house for us; Lord Melchett and Lord Erleigh and his wife Eva gave us a warm welcome and helped to introduce us to the world of English art and art connoisseurs.

My exhibition was very well received by the critics, although the material results were not as good as I had hoped. By the end of summer we embarked for the United States, where I was to meet Esther's parents and the rest of her family, whom I did not know at all. Her parents, her sister, her brother, all accepted me as a member of the family from the start. But I think they got something of a shock when they saw the wild-looking man, so different from the members of their circle, whom their beautiful Esther had married.

Again I met many of my old friends such as George Hellman and Alfred Stieglitz. But the general atmosphere was very different from that of 1928. There had been a great change in American life after the big crash in 1929. There was no longer prosperity as on my last visit, but depression. Formerly well-to-do people were now selling apples in the street to make a little money, and long lines waited at the free soup kitchens. Unemployment was rife and the bottom had dropped out of the art world. It was certainly not the best time for a painter to come to New York.

I took a studio in a pleasant neighborhood and tried to paint, but I did not have much heart for it. Esther, with love and devotion, tried to lessen the depression's effects upon me, and I tried to face up to the situation but I did not know how we would manage.

George Hellman, however, was encouraging and succeeded in arranging an exhibition for me at the Montross Gallery, a fine Fifth Avenue gallery. But there was nothing of the spirit or exhilaration of 1928. People talked mostly of their financial difficulties and appeared to wonder why art galleries still bothered to arrange exhibitions. A few paintings were sold to collectors but I felt it was time to leave. An exhibition was proposed for Chicago, but that would have meant staying on for another year, and I had lost the zest for fighting for recognition in a strange country. So we packed up our belongings and returned to Palestine.

RIDERS IN THE NEGEV 1960 *lithograph* From Album, Visages d'Israel Jacomet, Paris

Our honeymoon year was over. At home in Tel Aviv the economic situation was no better than in America, but my orange grove was blossoming and developing. It required more funds, but the supervisor managed to cover expenses and obtained credit for me in the hope of better days to come. We made a start of married life in our home, which overlooked the Mediterranean.

Sabbath mornings became our "at home day" and Esther's talent for entertaining and her easy, cordial hospitality gradually made our house a focal point for writers, artists, actors, musicians. They all started to make weekly pilgrimages to our apartment. The great poet Bialik was a regular visitor.

At this time I concentrated on stage designing for two theatres, the Habimah and the Ohel, which had in the meantime established themselves in the life of the country. The high spirits and dedication of these groups of actors made it an exciting experience to work for them and my mind was taken away from my own worries about the depression. It was at about this time that Marc Chagall, with his first wife Bella and their daughter Ida, made his first trip to Palestine. I was asked to show them around the country and I remember that while one could see that the landscape pleased him, it clearly did not have for him the attraction of Vitebsk.

There were difficult years insofar as my painting was concerned. Looking back, it seems that between 1932 and 1934 I painted very few works. The landscape painting that I had attacked with such spirit and enthusiasm a few years previously came to a stop. I did not seem able to regain the spirit of joy which had then animated me, and work for the theatre assumed more importance for me at this time. But by the end of 1932 a new project appeared to which I could devote my energies.

PEACE OFFERING 1955 *oil on canvas* 46 × 35 collection, Mr. Alex J. Weinstein, New York

WHITE ROSES 1965 *oil on canvas* 44 × 37   collection, Mr. and Mrs. Marcel Guggenheim, Zurich

Tel Aviv Gets an Art Museum

One day I was having a friendly glass of tea at the home of the Mayor of Tel Aviv, the ebullient Meir Dizengoff. A hearty, lively person, always full of optimism, he started to talk about an art museum for Tel Aviv. He had no knowledge of art whatsoever, but he did have a very fatherly feeling for his city in his ingenious way. He said to me, "Rubin, as you can see, we have everything in Tel Aviv now. We have schools, a hospital, a fire brigade, police, even a prison. But there is one thing we haven't got yet—an art museum."

Meir Dizengoff came from Russia and was trained as an engineer; art and its development were not his province. When he spoke about a museum for our partially-developed city of Tel Aviv, I started to laugh. But although the Mayor's ideas often seemed laughable, they had a way of turning into realities.

He continued seriously: "Let us make a museum. I'll give my house as the premises and you'll arrange it all."

No argument of mine could make him change his mind. He wanted to give up his home at once and hand it over to me for transformation into a museum. When I asked him where he proposed to live, he answered, "Well, I can reserve a corner for myself."

I told him that he would not be able to eat and sleep in a museum and he thereupon said that he would build a couple of rooms for his own use on the roof and the rest of the house would be the museum. The ground floor was occupied by a bank and he decided that the bank should be asked to leave so that his plan could be put into operation.

Mr. Dizengoff did build an apartment for himself on the roof and then, with the help of his loyal secretary, Itzhak Katz, I began to have the house cleaned, repainted, repaired, and the lighting rearranged. The Mayor's idea was that the museum should open with an exhibition of my works.

Only a few months after our conversation at tea the premises were ready. I hung my paintings in the second floor rooms and invitations were sent out for the opening. People came not only to see the exhibition but also to help the Mayor create a foundation for the future development of the museum. Baron de Menasce, for example, came all the way from Egypt. The opening of the museum in Tel Aviv was a dramatic moment for all those interested in art, especially for myself, who had arranged the first exhibition in the Citadel of David in Jerusalem in 1924. Large crowds came to the exhibition, not only to see my paintings but because Tel Avivians love anything new and they all wanted to see what a museum was like.

The first steps in the creation of the Tel Aviv Museum were not lacking in comic element. Mayor Dizengoff had many talks with me about the plans for the museum. He decided to go to Europe himself to solicit contributions from old friends, either in the form of money or works of art. When he talked about purchasing art I had to hide a smile, for on this subject he was quite ignorant. But I had too much respect for him to make any comment.

Mr. Dizengoff did manage to collect both funds and works on his European trip and when he returned to Tel Aviv he told me proudly that he had bought some "wonderful sculpture." For his Jewish museum he wanted to have the "Moses" of Michelangelo and the "David" of Donatello, and when he learned it was not possible to acquire the originals, he bought small bronze copies. I explained that it is not proper to put such objects in a museum: it must house original works of artistic value, either by contemporary artists or, if they can be obtained, by old masters.

Undaunted, he said, "When the cases arrive, you'll be able to see for yourself what I have bought." When the cases were opened, there were a two-foot high Moses and David of the type that is sold by the thousands all over Rome. Mr. Dizengoff finally understood he had made a mistake and had the pieces taken up to his own apartment. But he still had friends, he said, who would give him original works. And, in fact, from a friend in Belgium he did obtain good works by Ensor, Utrillo and Vlaminck.

Mr. Dizengoff stood the two pieces of sculpture on his roof-terrace, Moses at one side, David at the other. One summer night when there was a full moon, the Tel Aviv chief of police was walking on the roof of the police station, which was just opposite the Mayor's house. He looked across and saw what he took to be a man crouching on the roof, waiting to attack the Mayor. Quickly the efficient police came over and one of them, with a big stick, whammed Moses on the head, breaking his horns! Hearing the noise Mr. Dizengoff ran out in his pajamas and looked at the policeman in astonishment. "I thought somebody was coming to murder you," said the policeman. "But this is Moses by Michelangelo," replied Mr. Dizengoff, "and even without horns, he is going to remain in my house."

America's Wall Street crash had affected the whole world and the period of the early thirties was not an encouraging time for a painter in which to create, especially in Palestine, far away from art centers. I traveled a great deal about the country making innumerable sketches of the landscape, and tried to support myself and Esther by my work in theatres. The Habimah was my special interest and I constantly had in mind the possibility of obtaining funds so that a permanent building could be erected for this fine troupe.

One evening, when friends from abroad were visiting, among them Lord Melchett and the Baron de Menasce, I brought them to the cellar of the old Mograbi Theatre (then in the center of Tel Aviv) to see a certain play which the Habimah troupe was performing. The guests were greatly impressed by the high level of acting. During intermission, I mounted the stage and addressed the audience, referring to the distinguished guests present and pointing out how important it was to create a fund with which to build an adequate theatre to serve the needs of this remarkable theatrical company. My words found an echo and considerable sums of money were collected. In this way the Habimah building fund was started.

At that time the British High Commissioner was Sir Arthur Wauchope, a very fine gentleman, a lover of Palestine, and a sincere admirer of the efforts of the Jewish community to redeem the land and its culture. I had met him several times and our relationship was most cordial. He heard about the setting up of the building fund and expressed an interest in it. Although he knew no Hebrew, he was an admirer of Habimah, especially its star, the beautiful Hanna Rovina. One day an invitation arrived for Esther and me to spend a weekend at Government House in Jerusalem. We were delighted to accept. After the Saturday evening dinner party, I sat with Sir Arthur and we discussed the plan of building a theatre for Habimah and, generally, of creating a cultural center for Tel Aviv. In the course of our conversation the High Commissioner asked me to get up earlier than the other guests the next morning, so that I could attend with him the ceremony of the "Changing of the Colors," which took place every Sunday at eight in the morning. For me, a one-time immigrant from eastern Europe with its anti-Semitic atmosphere, it was a strange experience to stand with the High Commissioner for Palestine in the crisp morning air, viewing with him this Salute to the Colors. It was an episode I certainly could never have dreamed of in the Rumanian ghetto. Doubtless he thought that by showing me this special favor he was promoting the development of art—in his way.

Returning to the residency, Sir Arthur took my arm and said that he would like to do something concrete about the project we had discussed the night before. He asked me what could be of practical value. I replied that it would be a very fine gesture if the Mandatory Government could requisition a plot of land in Tel Aviv as the site for a cultural center, which should comprise a theatre, library, and, eventually, a concert hall. The High Commissioner said that he thought it was an idea that should be given consideration.

Two weeks later, the District Commissioner in Jaffa, Mr. Crosbie, told me that he had received orders from the High Commissioner to requisition a 20-*dunam* (five acres) plot of land and he showed me on the map approximately where the land lay. It consisted of some dried-up orange groves outside the city limits, the home of jackals that used to howl every night. I was rather horrified that we should have to accept such a piece of land and said something to this effect. However, the decision became definite and a date was set for the High Commissioner to come to Tel Aviv for the formal transfer of the land. Sir Arthur was of the opinion that Tel Aviv would soon expand beyond these orange groves and that the spot would later become a center of the city. In the presence of the Habimah actors and actresses and some of the public and the then Mayor of Tel Aviv, the late Israel Rokach, and other dignitaries, the deed was signed as a gift to the city of Tel Aviv for the purpose of erecting a cultural center on the site.

My remark, that nobody would come to a theater so far away, was met with laughter, but it did seem at the time that the location was most unsuitable. Today I can see how farsighted Sir Arthur Wauchope was, for now this spot houses not only the Habimah Theatre but also the Helena Rubinstein Pavilion of the Tel Aviv Museum and the fine Frederic R. Mann Auditorium, surrounded by a well laid-out garden. The whole complex forms the most attractive center of greater Tel Aviv.

In 1936 there was yet another outbreak of Arab riots, which started in Jaffa and spread throughout the country. Again bloodshed and violence. Nonsensical as it seemed at that particular time, I decided that I would hold an exhibition in Jerusalem. It was my way of fighting the gloom created by the situation. I induced a small bookshop owner, Steimatsky, to take part in the "adventure" and to renovate a couple of his rooms so that the exhibition could be held in pleasant surroundings. Sir Arthur Wauchope was encouraging and the exhibition was opened under his patronage and in his presence. Depressed Jerusalem welcomed the event like an unexpected gift. In spite of the general situation the show was well received, with many visitors and good sales.

Nineteen thirty-six was also the year in which I met Bronislaw Huberman, who came to Palestine filled with enthusiasm over his plan to create a symphony orchestra made up mainly of displaced Jewish musicians from central Europe. A man of vision and tremendous energy as well as a great violinist, he did not permit his plans for the future to be disturbed by events of the present. There was, of course, no adequate concert hall and twenty years were to elapse before one was built. But Huberman leased one of the exhibition halls of the Levant Fair near the port of Tel Aviv and had it converted into a concert hall.

Soon we heard that the great Toscanini himself was coming to conduct the opening concert. A concert by a new orchestra conducted by Toscanini! The whole country was fired with enthusiasm, augmented by the fact that it was a country torn by riots. December 26th, the great day of the opening concert: I still recall the emotion that filled the hall when onto the platform stepped the erect, lively figure of Toscanini, and the first notes sounded. I was sitting next to Dr. Judah Magnes, the then rector of the Hebrew University of Jerusalem, and I could see the tears in his eyes. And, indeed, many people were moved. The music revealed a heaven of hope among the dark clouds of the continuous tension in which we lived in Palestine.

Later, I got to know Toscanini and his charming and efficient wife Carla, and a warm friendship developed between us as well as with Wanda, his daughter, and Vladimir Horowitz, her husband. I went to Jerusalem with the meastro and I can still remember the three rainbows we saw on the way. Toscanini said that he must get out of the car to say a prayer, and

MAESTRO TOSCANINI 1936 *drawing, pen and ink* collection of the artist

he walked along the road, muddy after the rain, in his small patent leather shoes as if he were walking on air.

While the plans for the building of the Habimah Theatre still continued, by the spring of 1937 the committee found that they could not proceed with the work, owing to lack of funds; a substantial loan was needed. There was only one place where it could be raised: London. Of all people, the committee chose me to go to London to try to arrange the loan; they seemed to believe I could manage anything. I agreed, as I did not like to disappoint them, but I had no idea how to set about negotiating such a loan. The question of my traveling expenses and maintenance in London was never even mentioned.

Taking with me a number of watercolors which I had painted in the last few years. I went to London to win financial support for a Hebrew theatre in Palestine! Sensible people must have thought the whole project completely foolhardy. But since the Arthur Tooth Gallery had already arranged two exhibitions for me, I took my watercolors to them and explained the situation. The gallery took the watercolors and, without a special exhibition, sold all of them to various collectors. With the few hundred pounds thus received, I felt myself a man of means and I commenced my round of visits to the great financial figures of London.

200

The money-men looked with a pitying smile at the artist who had come to London to raise a loan for a theatre in half-built Tel Aviv. But I had the good luck to contact a certain man in the financial world who did not find the idea ridiculous but took it seriously and decided to send a representative to Tel Aviv to look into the affair. So I was able to return happily to Tel Aviv, and the special agent sent from London duly worked out the details for the loan.

Back in Tel Aviv I was full of plans for future exhibitions; I had tentatively set a date with the Tooth Gallery for another show in 1940 or 1941. The Nazi persecution of the Jews in Germany was gaining momentum; refugees, including a number of painters, had already arrived in Palestine but I still went ahead with my plans for the future.

At the beginning of 1938 I received letters from old friends in Rumania, which I had not visited for some fifteen years, suggesting that I hold an exhibition there, as they were sure that I would have a wonderful reception and be successful. A friend of mine, who was a refugee from Nazi Germany, Professor Oscar Kaufmann, was a noted Berlin architect and had designed the Habimah Theatre building. He also had received an invitation from Rumania to design a house for a business tycoon there. Professor Kaufmann too urged me to come, saying that he would commission me to do a mural for the house. The idea began to interest me. Then the Rumanian Consul General called on me to say that he had received word from Bucharest about my projected visit, and he suggested that the opportunity be used for me to execute stage designs for the new opera that was going to be presented at Christmas, 1939, under the auspices of the King.

Suddenly, I found myself in the midst of preparations for an exhibition, a mural, and for stage designs for an opera, which dealt with the life of Mary Magdalena and, therefore, had connections with the Holy Land. All these unexpected projects gave me the usual strong drive to work, making those demands on me which caused my artist's imagination to stir.

I was interested in the Rumanian visit for another reason: Esther had often heard me speak of my childhood and youth there and she was eager to see the place where my youthful dreams had been born. By the beginning of July, 1939, all preparations were made. We decided to leave in August and spend about six months in Rumania.

One August morning, I awoke and told Esther that I had a strong feeling against going to Europe, for I had dreamt that our old synagogue in Falticeni was burning. I have always believed in signs and portents, and even today seldom undertake a new venture without opening my Bible blindfolded and reading the passage my hand falls upon, as a guide. So I was not prepared to pass over lightly the implications of my dream. I asked Esther to allow me to postpone the trip for a fortnight and then, if nothing happened in the meantime, we would leave. It was during these two weeks that war erupted and, of course, our plan to go to Rumania was abandoned.

I sat on my cases of paintings like the Jews of the Bible by the waters of Babylon and wondered what I should do now. There seemed to be no sense either in starting on fresh paintings or staying in Tel Aviv. For my mind was set on traveling, and everything was prepared for our departure. So we decided that we would switch our plans from Rumania to New York and see what the future would bring.

We booked passage on a ship that went to Marseilles and thence to New York, a long journey. The sea seemed to be at war also, and our trip was marked by stormy weather. We had to stay twenty-four hours in Marseilles, so I went into the town to try and hear what was being said about the political situation. There seemed to be complete apathy; people did not believe that the war would develop or that the civilian population would be affected. I was glad to board the ship again and leave behind me the grey atmosphere of Europe.

In New York, life went on normally. Nobody spoke of the war or even wanted to hear about it. The general feeling seemed to be that they had been drawn into a European war once before and were not going to allow it to happen again. This was not their war; it did not concern America. I somehow had the feeling that we would not be able to return to Palestine for some time and set about finding a place to stay. We had the good fortune to find two rooms on the sixth floor of an old building in the center of Manhattan, at the corner of 58th Street and Madison Avenue. There was a good view of the city, and downstairs there was a drug store with a lunch counter. I liked to have my midday meal here, with the people coming in from the street for a quick lunch—janitors, postmen, truck drivers. The food was simple but good. Nearby was a small, basement movie house which showed old films, and there I was able to relax. Every day Esther and I walked in nearby Central Park, enjoying the air and the sight of children at play in the big city.

Living in the middle of the big, noisy city with its many art galleries. and constant change of exhibitions, acted as a goad to my creativity. Nineteen-forty was a time of intense productivity. I began to feel myself part of the New York art scene. Materially my situation was far from good, and although we lived economically, life in New York was an expensive affair. But by the spring, an exhibition was arranged by the Milch Gallery which aroused considerable attention, and Alfred Barr, Jr., director of the new Museum of Modern Art came twice to see my works. He selected the "Flute Player" for the permanent collection of the museum and Mrs. Felix Warburg presented it as a gift. The results of the exhibition were both artistically and financially satisfactory, and when the Museum of Modern Art opened a show of new acquisitions, I was happy to see my painting prominently displayed, while the *New York Times* gave a good place to a favorable review of my canvas.

At this time I received an unexpected compliment from a great art dealer and connoisseur, Georges Wildenstein, whom I did not even know personally. A lady came to my exhibition saying that since she wanted a

MUSICAL INTERLUDE: HOMAGE TO CASALS   1964   *oil on canvas*   36 × 29   CASALS   collection Norton Gallery, Palm Beach, Gift of Regenstein Foundation

flower painting and did not want to pay the price of a Redon or a Renoir, Mr. Wildenstein had advised her to acquire a Rubin, and in this way I sold an important canvas.

My show at the Milch Gallery also brought me into contact with an art dealer from the West Coast, Dalzell Hatfield of Los Angeles, who had come to New York on business. He was a lively, energetic man, with a quick and discriminating eye. We soon became very friendly and from that time on the Hatfield Gallery in Los Angeles became my West Coast representative. Mr. Hatfield and his wife were most charming and warm-hearted—typical Americans in the best sense of the term.

In the meantime, the effects of the European war began to make themselves felt in the United States, and strong feelings started to rise against Hitler's barbarities. Then the tragedy of Pearl Harbor brought home to Americans the full horror of war, and they realized that the time for action had come. Normal activities, however, continued in the art world, and Esther and I went to California for the exhibition that had been arranged at the Hatfield Gallery. California, with its beauty, mild climate, its vegetation and orange groves, reminded me of Palestine.

My exhibition was a success and also gave me the opportunity of meeting such personalities as Arthur Rubinstein and Edward G. Robinson, and of renewing my acquaintance with Jashcha Heifetz, Vladimir Horo-witz, and the Toscaninis, the latter whom we later visited in their summer home. Particularly I remember the meeting with Arthur Rubinstein, who came to the exhibition with his beautiful wife Nella. Although she was pregnant at the time, they came all the way from their Beverly Hills home, which meant, because of the restrictions on the use of private cars, they had to take two different buses. Meeting this great musician and most delightful of human beings with his lovely, serene wife, and being admitted to their intimate circle, I consider one of the greatest acquisitions of that stay in California.

Esther and I were also the guests of our dear friends Rudy and Pauline Polk in their charming Beverly Hills home where prominent musicians used to gather. There we passed some enjoyable and relaxing months, meeting, among others, the great comedienne Fanny Brice, who was also an art lover. Through her I learned of the world of theatre and television and I especially recall how much I enjoyed the lively company of Charles Laughton, his wife Elsa Lanchester, writer Marc Connelly, and others. The friendships from that period have continued till today and are among my precious possessions.

In 1942 I returned to New York with Esther, who had in the mean-time joined the A.W.V.S. (American Women's Voluntary Service) and was much occupied with her war work. With the advancement of the war, the general atmosphere became much more serious and tense. I spent most of my time at my easel, or walking through Central Park, where I made friends with the squirrels who recognized me and waited daily for me to come and feed them.

THE OLD VIOLINIST 1967 *oil on canvas* 23 × 15½ collection, Rosenfeld Gallery, Tel Aviv

In 1944 the Hatfield Gallery invited me to hold another exhibition, and again Esther and I went to California. It was while riding in a car there with Rubinstein that I heard the radio announcing the landing in Normandy. My exhibition opened in an atmosphere of hope and high spirits. While meeting the many friends we had made on our previous visit, we felt as if we were returning to the bosom of a huge family. We were greeted on all sides with heart-warming friendship. The material results of the exhibition were most encouraging; Esther and I, already married for fifteen years, began to think about raising a family. When we left California, Esther was carrying my son David, who was born in New York in the spring of 1945, just as peace was in sight.

Back in New York we fell into the pattern of our old life again, becoming very friendly with a number of refugees from France, such as the family of the Baron Edouard de Rothschild, and seeing such artists as Marc Chagall, Moise Kisling and Ossip Zadkine. Now that Esther was going to have a child, we were faced with the problem of finding a larger apartment. Eventually we found what we wanted, on Central Park South in a building that overlooked Columbus Circle.

It was a beautiful spring day, April 3, 1945, when at six o'clock in the morning I came back from the hospital with our good friend, Dr. Rongy, the well-known obstetrician, who had delivered my son. I, who generally worried about financial matters and always foresaw difficulties, met the appearance of a costly new addition to the family with complete confidence. I felt exalted, as if a ray of pure light had come into my life. The question of where the money would come from to meet my new responsibilities did not trouble me this time.

It had been an old dream of mine that if ever I should have a son, he should be called "David," for in the Middle Ages there had been a David Hareuveni in Italy whose dream it was to create a Jewish state in Palestine. And so my son was named David Hareuveni, with the memory of my Italian hero in mind. And only three years after David's birth, the Jewish state came into being.

In our New York apartment we welcomed many of the Palestinians who were coming to the United States to try to obtain support for the Jewish underground. This organization's aim was to enable every Jew who wanted to go to Palestine to be able to do so, in spite of the British White Paper on immigration. I particularly remember the tea party we gave for Moshe Shertok, who later became Israel's first Foreign Minister, changing his name to "Sharett," and Yaacov Dostrovsky, who later became the first Chief of Staff of the Israel Army, changing his name to "Dori." We had invited not only wealthy American Jews to meet them but also some of the French refugees and artists and writers. Introducing Moshe Shertok I said quite naturally, "our future Foreign Secretary," for I was convinced even then that the destruction and sufferings of European Jewry would find their indemnity in the creation of a Jewish state in Palestine. The prophets had said that the Messiah would come after great

RABBI WITH TORAH 1966 *oil on canvas* 36 × 24 collection, Mr. and Mrs. Sidney Baer, Philadelphia

sufferings, and for me the coming of the Messiah meant the creation of a Jewish state where Jews would be able to live in freedom and dignity.

The arrival of David, the third member of our family, with the great happiness it brought, had its effect not only on my work but also on my way of working. I now worked with ease, optimistically, and the hours flew by. Emotions that I had lacked for so many years now came to the surface as I looked at my little son with his pale gold hair and blue eyes like a Botticelli angel. The end of the war, the crushing of Hitlerism, and my private happiness aroused such intense feeling in me that there were times when I felt like shouting aloud for joy. But there was one more element missing that our family happiness required: Our return to Palestine.

Up to the beginning of 1946 there was no possibility of traveling through the Mediterranean, but as soon as it was announced that a former troop ship was carrying passengers to the east Mediterranean ports of Alexandria, Haifa and Beirut, I took passage for the family. Accommodation on the ship was extremely poor; we had to bring hammocks and folding beds on which to sleep. The big problem was food for a one-year-old child. But the ship's staff and crew were delighted to have a baby passenger on their first civilian trip. The little boy was received with open arms and his food was stored on ice. Our David was the center of attention and was even brought to the captain's table.

En route we were disappointed to learn that the ship would not dock at Haifa as expected, and we would have to disembark at Alexandria. Fortunately our old friend Georges de Menasce had a house there and was waiting for us when we landed. We had a few days' rest in his home and, with his help, planned our trip to Tel Aviv. A sleeper was booked on the train running through the desert to Kantara—a trip which took about thirty hours. It was an unpleasant journey, with our compartment filled with noisy Arab women and children, and, to our discomfort, a dust storm blew up. When at last we arrived in Tel Aviv the whole little family was completely exhausted and, to our dismay, we had no place to stay. Our old apartment was occupied by other tenants, so we went to the village of Bnei Brak, on the outskirts of Tel Aviv, where my brother lived.

The return to Palestine, which we had left six years before and to which Esther and I had been so eagerly looking forward, turned out to be disappointing. The war had left the country in a state of turmoil; there was great political unrest and constant disturbances. Food was still rationed and accommodation was very difficult to find. We decided to go to Jerusalem and take the first place we could find which happened to be a house belonging to a couple who had gone to England for a few months. At least we had a roof over our heads, but the atmosphere, with constant shooting incidents and bombings, was not favorable to work, and I could not concentrate on painting. Among the Jewish community the feeling was growing stronger and stronger toward one aim: independence.

Eventually we were able to rent an apartment in Tel Aviv and I started working again. Then, in November, 1947, the United Nations

BIBLICAL VISION 1966 *oil on canvas* 32 × 26 collection of the artist

Assembly approved the partition of Palestine. The Jewish community went mad with joy and excitement. Crowds danced in the street, singing "Hatikva" and weeping with happiness and hope.

But the U.N. resolution was the signal for the most violent Arab attacks the country had known. They started to kill, burn, destroy, loot. The street where we lived became part of the front line; we became accustomed to the sound of bullets and bombs. One side of our house was constantly exposed to the bullets of the snipers from Jaffa. We had one room with a partition and behind this I put my easel and, strangely enough, found I was painting with renewed vigor while Esther, with her cool and collected behavior, helped keep the morale of the household high.

Then came May 14, 1948. The Jewish state, the State of Israel, for which a people without a home had waited two thousand years, had finally come into being! And then came the attacks from the encircling Arab nations—the armies of Egypt, Syria, Lebanon, Iraq, Jordan on the move against the tiny Israel enclave. I am a painter and not a writer and I lack the words that can express the exaltation, the greatness of that historic time. All I know is that not for anything in the world would I have missed living through those heart-stirring, glorious days.

For me personally, the apogee of the declaration of the State of Israel came when the Provisional Government appointed me the first Minister Plenipotentiary to Rumania.

ARAB HORSES 1966 *drawing, pen and ink* private collection, London   SNAKE CHARMER 1966 *drawing, pen and ink* collection, Ohana Gallery, London

In Israel's Diplomatic Service

It was a most unexpected appointment; I had never thought about being a diplomat. Then one morning I got a telephone call from the then Minister for Foreign Affairs, Moshe Sharett, telling me that he would like to see me. Completely unaware of what was awaiting me, I remember jokingly asking him whether, now that he was a minister, did he want me to paint his portrait? But Sharett only repeated that he wanted to see me. Accordingly, I called on him.

"You know," he said, "we had a meeting of the new government and it has been decided to send ministers and ambassadors to various countries where we need them badly. One of these countries is Rumania and we want you to be our minister in Bucharest. How do you feel about it?"

I looked at him rather blankly and said, "I can't answer you on the spot. It is so unexpected. But I'll go home and think about it and give you my answer tomorrow." Then I asked him what made him think of me, as I am not a diplomat. The Foreign Minister answered that he thought I would make a good diplomat and would know what to do, in the same way that I had known what to do in my painting career.

After giving the matter considerable thought, I told him the next day that I would be pleased to accept the appointment and serve my country and my people. Thereafter we met several times and I was told in detail what my mission would be.

This appointment represented an important milestone in my life. I had left the land of my birth a poor, struggling, would-be painter and I was about to return to it as an accredited representative of the new state. It was an extraordinary moment for me and I vowed that I would do my very utmost to prove worthy of the trust reposed in me. I managed to get hold of all the books and pamphlets on diplomacy and protocol that I could, and I studied them thoroughly. I knew that there would be exceptional problems for me to face and try to solve, first and foremost being the opening of the door which would permit the Jews of Rumania to emigrate to Israel. I must confess that my thoughts often turned to another painter, one of the greatest, Peter Paul Rubens, who likewise had been called upon to serve as ambassador for his country. I prayed that I too would be successful in my mission.

JERUSALEM, THE HOLY CITY 1964 *oil on canvas* 26 × 32 Hallmark collection, Kansas City

SIMHAT TORAH   1967   *oil on canvas*   32 × 26   collection, Mr. and Mrs. Leslie Jackson, London

At the beginning of November, 1948, I set off with my wife, our three-and-a-half-year-old son, and the staff allocated to me, in a chartered plane. The trip to Bucharest, which should have taken about four hours, lasted three days. This seemed to be the usual case with trips to eastern Europe, and no logical explanation was forthcoming. It was just a state of affairs that had to be accepted. The appearance in Rumania of a diplomat from Israel in the person of a painter was well received. It may be that I was even helped by the nature of my true calling, for if I was gauche or on occasion undiplomatic, the tendency was to find an excuse, because "one knows what artists are . . ."

The Jewish community in Rumania could not contain its joy and excitement at seeing a living symbol of the new State of Israel and, more-over, a symbol that was personified by someone who had sprung from the same soil as themselves. I had the impression that these people, who had suffered so much from the Nazis during the war and had gone through years of hunger and deprivation, were looking toward the Israeli repre-sentative as a "savior," a sort of Messiah who would solve all their prob-lems and put an end to all their troubles. There were many times when I felt I was living the life of some other person.

The official Israeli residence was a fine house with a beautiful garden and splendid rooms in one of the best sections of Bucharest. I had brought my painting materials with me if I should have time to paint, but for the whole eighteen months of my service, and indeed, for some time after-ward, I did not put brush to canvas. The work of the legation absorbed me completely.

It took me some months to accustom myself to my new duties and I was fortunate in having the support and aid of my wife and a competent staff. I do not intend to treat of the political aspects of my work but will only mention certain events that illustrate the particular atmosphere in which the Israeli Mission then lived, an atmosphere that had a spiritual significance to me.

The large Jewish community of Bucharest was anxious to see more of the Israel envoy and his family and to come in closer contact with our legation. I tried to avoid such close contact, believing it would have unfavorable repercussions not only on the work of our mission but on the Jewish community itself. When, however, the head of the Jewish com-munity requested that we come to the great synagogue on a particular Sabbath when hundreds of Jews would be gathered there, it seemed to me that there was no harm in gratifying such a desire. But the event was so widely publicized that I realized there would be not hundreds of our co-religionists, but thousands, and an unruly demonstration might result. A diplomatic indisposition served as an excuse to be absent. The following Sabbath, however, without any prior notice, Esther, my staff and I walked to the synagogue for the morning service. No sooner did a few people see us walking in the direction of the synagogue than crowds started to collect

FLUTE PLAYER 1958 *oil on canvas* 36 × 24 collection, Mr. and Mrs. Josef Rosensaft, New York

Overleaf: SUNSET IN THE NEGEV 1962/63 *oil on canvas* 50½ × 64 collection, Mr. and Mrs. Louis Regenstein, Jr. Atlanta

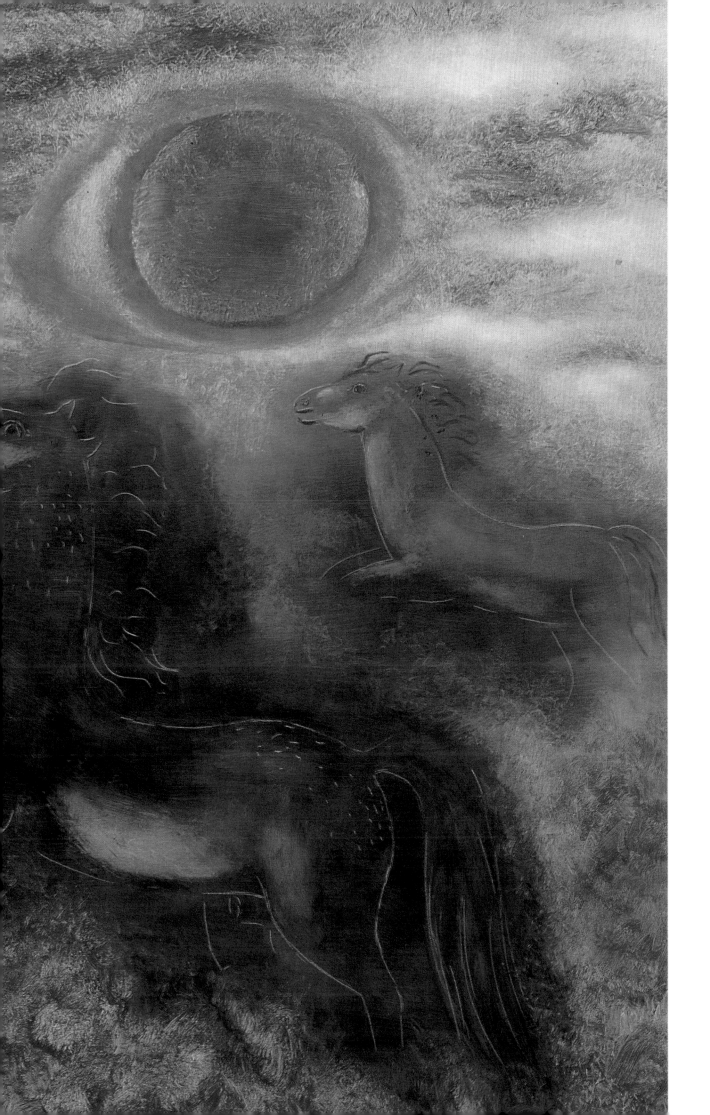

outside the building. The service started in a tense, electric atmosphere. The climax came when I was asked to take the scroll of the Law from the ark, an honor always given to a distinguished member of the congregation. People fell upon their knees or stretched themselves out on the floor and I was unable to proceed. I could not make them resume their places and literally had to walk to the reading desk over prostrate bodies. When I I came to read the portion of the Bible selected for that particular Sabbath, there was an explosion of murmurs, groans and tears from the whole assembly, for the passage began: "Get thee unto Pharaoh in the morning . . . And thou shalt say unto him, the Lord God of the Hebrews hath sent me unto thee, saying, Let my people go . . ." (Exodus, Chapter 7, Verses 15–16.)

That this should have been the chapter to be read just on the Sabbath I came to the synagogue seemed to me more than a strange coincidence. It was an amazing experience to live through and, even now, after twenty years, I cannot think of it without a chill running through my body.

Besides the continuous administrative and diplomatic duties there were some moving moments when I met friends of my youth again. Especially touching was the meeting with the old poet, Barbu Lazareanu, who, in the meantime, had become General Secretary of the Academy; and with the great novelist and poet, Mihail Sadovianu, the leading figure in modern Rumanian literature, who now was Vice President of the country.

The dominant desire which animated me was to find a way of enabling those Jews who wanted to go to Israel to be able to do so. This was the goal I never lost sight of, and it was a wonderful moment when, after ten months of unceasing efforts, the Rumanian Government finally recognized the right of Rumanian Jews to emigrate to Israel.

My mission had been far from easy. During the year and a half that it lasted, I had to accustom myself to living a totally different sort of life from my usual "life of an artist." My work demanded the expenditure of all my energies and kept me in a state of constant anxiety. It might have been even more difficult had I not established good relations with the Foreign Minister, the redoubtable Ana Pauker, with whom, naturally, I was more in contact than with any other political figure. Perhaps the outstanding woman in the political life of eastern Europe, she had a powerful intellect, an intimidating manner, and was known as "difficult."

On my very first visit to her, she said that I "was not unknown" to her. In 1917–18, I had been one of the organizers of a hostel in Bucharest for poor Jewish students. A number of young students worked there in various capacities to earn a little money. One of them, working as a waitress, was Ana Pauker, although she was not known under that name. She remembered me, rather than the other way around, doubtless because with my gaunt face, mop of black hair and general exotic appearance, I was rather noticeable. Whatever the cause, she seemed to have remembered me favorably, and personally I always found her approachable and understanding.

The first ship to leave for Israel, with a thousand immigrants on board, was the *Transylvania* and it was on this ship that my family and I returned to our home. I was buoyed up by the feeling that I had managed to do something important for my people and I thought how happy and proud my father would have been to know that his son had been instrumental in bringing Jews back to the Holy Land. But, as has been often said, no one is a prophet in his own country, and in Israel particularly, much is taken for granted. I had expected that I would be met in Haifa port by some high officials, as a sign of recognition of my work. There was not even a representative of the Foreign Office waiting to greet me. Later I was told that an official had been sent to meet me but that a minor car accident had prevented him from arriving in time. But I returned to my Tel Aviv home, a sadder if not a wiser man.

About a week later I went to Tiberias to see the Prime Minister, David Ben Gurion, who was taking a brief rest there. Not only was I an admirer of his, but we were old friends, and I always valued his quick, shrewd and penetrating reactions. When I described to him my life and efforts as Minister to Rumania and then, naively perhaps, told him of my disappointment at the "reception" I had on arrival and as always, while I was talking he made notes in the small notebook he inevitably carried with him, he looked up at me with his twinkling eyes and wise smile said, "Rubin, you're only a painter and you've got to be content with the reception you got. You should be happy that nobody threw stones at you." It was a philosophical remark from which I learned a good deal.

It was good to be home again, to receive greetings from so many old friends and to walk again along the seashore of Tel Aviv and through its streets. I was longing to take up my brush again, as hungry for painting as a starving man for food. But first I had to readjust mentally and forget my service as a diplomat. Jascha Heifetz came to Israel at this time to appear with the Israel Philharmonic, and listening to him make music calmed my mood as well as giving me deep pleasure. Music, especially in my latter years, has meant much to me and an inspiring concert has often resulted in my dashing to my easel and working with renewed spontaneity.

On this occasion, Heifetz bought a flower piece from me, taking it with him to Paris, where he was to give some concerts before continuing to New York. Some time later he told me what trouble the painting had given him. Seeing the canvas signed "Rubin," the customs official said that he must get in touch with the Louvre to ascertain whether it really was a "Rubens" (he had never, of course, heard of the Israel painter!), and no explanation from Heifetz would satisfy him. Finally, the violinist had to send the painting on straight to New York and could not carry it with him as he wished.

As a diplomat I had been a "dollar-a-year-man" and it now behoved me to set about really earning some money. Once more I began thinking

of a New York exhibition, since I had again received many invitations to show my paintings there. So, at the beginning of 1952, I went off to the United States with my family, letting my Tel Aviv apartment to some friends in the Foreign Office. In New York we found a place in the same house we had lived in during the war. This time I took a larger apartment as we were now three in the family, with a fourth member on the way. I always found it inspiring to work in the turmoil and noise of this corner of New York—58th Street and Madison Avenue. I felt again the stimulation given me by the feeling of "life" around me. At the end of the year, on the 13th of November, the date of my own birthday, my daughter Ariella was born—the most beautiful gift Esther could ever have presented me!

In 1953 I held a very good exhibition at the Grace Borgenicht Gallery in New York when I met some of the artists the gallery owner represented and especially remember Milton Avery, the personal quality of whose work I very much appreciated. The following year I had another show at the Hatfield Gallery in Los Angeles, which was again gratifyingly successful on all counts. Exhibitions in the Mint Museum in Charlotte, North Carolina, and the Tennessee Museum in Nashville also took place during this visit. Returning to Tel Aviv, I now had the means to purchase the house we had lived in and to build a fine, roomy studio on the roof where I could work peacefully, away from the distractions of the household.

Nineteen fifty-five saw the opening of a large retrospective exhibition at the Helena Rubinstein Pavilion of the Tel Aviv Museum, which had the special interest for me of bringing together early works that I myself had not seen for many years. Some time later I received an invitation from the fine Ohana Gallery in the West End of London, and on a beautiful spring day in May, 1957, an exhibition opened there. This was my fourth one-man show in London and proved very rewarding. Many collectors who already owned my paintings acquired additional works, and there were a number of new buyers as well.

In 1958 I took part in exhibitions of Israeli art at the Arts Council gallery in London and at the Museum of Modern Art in Paris, at which time the French Government acquired two of my paintings.

It was around this time that I was asked by the noted French publisher, Daniel Jacomet of Paris, to prepare a series of drawings for publication in album form. He selected a dozen drawings, mostly pen and wash, which were issued a couple of years later under the title of *Images d'Israel*, with an introduction by French critic Florent Fels and Dr. Haim Gamzu, director of the Tel Aviv Museum. The exquisite precision of the printing gave me personally a great deal of pleasure, while the 250 numbered copies of the album were quickly bought by collectors.

Passing through Paris I had the pleasure of again meeting my old friend Georges Wildenstein and his son Daniel, and was happy to be asked to exhibit in their New York Gallery on the occasion of my 70th birthday, which was still some three years off. I realized that this would be a very special sort of exhibition and started well in advance to gather together some of my old as well as new canvases.

When the time came for the exhibition and I saw my works hung in the beautiful, spacious Wildenstein Gallery, with its excellent lighting, I felt that I was really seeing my paintings for the first time.

I have had many exhibitions with crowded *vernissages*, but opening day at the Wildenstein was an unprecedented event for me. The gathering was tumultuous, with the crowd of visitors stretching far into the street. I could never have believed that in New York there existed so many people interested in seeing a Rubin show. The opening proved a good augury for the success of the exhibition, which was outstanding and certainly exceeded my greatest expectations. Georges Wildenstein arrived from Paris a few days before the exhibition closed and I very much enjoyed listening to his perceptive analysis of my work as we went through the show together.

Shortly after my New York visit, the imposing new Israel Museum in Jerusalem, with its interesting garden landscaped by Noguchi, gave me a big retrospective exhibition—the first one-man show of an Israeli artist in this museum—with a well-illustrated catalogue. The same show was repeated at the Tel Aviv Museum. These two exhibitions gave me a chance to meet and talk once again to many friends and acquaintances from my early years in the country. It was a nostalgic and moving experience. About this time, a Jerusalem dealer and publisher, Binet, came upon the twelve woodcuts, "The God Seekers," that I had done long before, in 1923. At that time there were no expert printers in Jerusalem and I had to undertake the entire printing myself. Mr. Binet took over the original blocks and issued a magnificent album. It was a great personal satisfaction to see my works of so many years ago coming alive again.

It was not till 1965 that I had my first exhibition in Switzerland, arranged by the enterprising and charming Mme. Marguerite Motte at her Geneva Gallery. This exhibition provided Esther and me with a wonderful opportunity of spending a delightful month in Switzerland, enjoying especially our visits to the various art collections, private as well as public, which are certainly one of the glories of that country. Another opportunity for a combined exhibition and holiday came with my show in Palm Beach, Florida, at the Norton Museum. The rich, lush green of the Florida landscape remained vividly in my mind when I returned to Tel Aviv in 1966, and its effect can be seen in my handling of this color now.

By this time, my Tel Aviv had become a huge metropolis with sand dunes, being replaced by the noise of a modern city. Even the Habimah Theatre, once on the far outskirts of the town, was right in the center. I felt that now, when I reached my seventies, I would like to dream again as in my youth. The open spaces, the sea, and the dunes were my first love that attracted me to live in Israel. It was this, and even more, that I discovered in Caesarea, on the shores of the Mediterranean. Ruins of an ancient past filled the unspoiled natural beauty of the place. And on a hill, overlooking the old Roman aqueduct, I built my dream-house and studio. And thus,

PEACE OFFERING 1967 *oil on canvas* 36 × 29 collection of the artist

yearnings expressed in my youth poems over fifty years ago, finally came true.

On shores of sea, I build thee my home,

To wash your tired feet,

In golden foam of green and blues . . .

In all the years that I have lived in Israel I never remember a time when there was no tension, yet this seldom affected my desire and capability to paint. I can remember that during the War of Independence I painted some of my gayest flower pieces. But when the dark clouds started to gather again in the early summer of 1967, I could not touch a brush. I felt overwhelmed by forebodings. Perhaps this time because my son was in the army and the house felt so empty without him. The days before the actual outbreak on June 5th were days filled with menace and dread, and life seemed to have come to a standstill. Esther, as usual, awaited whatever might come with stoic calm, and imbued our home with her steadfastness of spirit. Only two days before the actual start of the Six Day War, my son David came home in a mood of pent-up excitement. He said to me, "Daddy, you always like to read the Bible to find an answer to your problems in it. Why don't you look in the Bible now, for me, and tell me what is going to happen to us all?" I asked my little daughter to bring me the Bible and I asked David to open it, and, without looking, to put his finger on a page. He opened at Leviticus, Chapter 26, Verse 6. Here it is:

"And I will give peace in the land, and ye shall

lie down, and none shall make you afraid: and I

will rid evil beasts out of the land, neither

shall the sword go through your land.

"And ye shall chase your enemies, and they

shall fall before you by the sword.

"And five of you shall chase a hundred, and

a hundred of you shall put ten thousand to

flight; and your enemies shall fall before

you by the sword."

Our spirits soared at God's word. . . .

ROOSTER *drawing, pen and ink*   From Album, Visages d'Israel Jacomet, Paris

List of Paintings

★   Color illustration